THEOLOGY AND THE KINGDOM OF GOD

BOOKS BY WOLFHART PANNENBERG
Published by The Westminster Press

Theology and the Kingdom of God
Jesus – God and Man

THEOLOGY
AND THE
KINGDOM
OF GOD

by
WOLFHART
PANNENBERG

Edited by
Richard John Neuhaus

THE WESTMINSTER PRESS
Philadelphia

Grateful acknowledgment is made to The Macmillan Company, Macmillan & Co., Ltd., Macmillan Co. of Canada, Ltd., and Michael Yeats, for permission to reprint lines from " The Second Coming," in *Collected Poems,* by William Butler Yeats. Copyright 1924 by The Macmillan Company, renewed 1952 by Bertha Georgie Yeats.

STANDARD BOOK NO. 664–24842–X

LIBRARY OF CONGRESS CATALOG CARD NO. 69–12668

Published by The Westminster Press ®
Philadelphia, Pennsylvania

PRINTED IN THE UNITED STATES OF AMERICA

6   7   8   9   10   11   12

ACKNOWLEDGMENTS

Grateful acknowledgment is made to the following:

Una Sancta, Inc., for the articles from *Una Sancta,* an ecumenical journal of theology for Christian renewal: "Theology and the Kingdom of God," Vol. 24, No. 2, Pentecost, 1967; "The Kingdom of God and the Church," Vol. 24, No. 4, Christmass, 1967; and "The Kingdom of God and the Foundation of Ethics," Vol. 25, No. 2, Pentecost, 1968.

American Academy of Religion, for "Appearance as the Arrival of the Future," *Journal of the American Academy of Religion,* Vol. XXXV, No. 2, June, 1967.

CONTENTS

WOLFHART PANNENBERG:
PROFILE OF A THEOLOGIAN

One promising spring morning in 1968, page one of *The New York Times* brought the news. The " death of God " thing was out. The theology of hope was in. The change was generally welcomed. After relentless months of moral tragedy in Vietnam, after the almost orgiastic periods of national self-denigration over violence and the torturing of the cities, people were ready for something more optimistic. In previous weeks the religious fashion editors of *Time* and *Newsweek* had signaled the switch with feature previews of Jürgen Moltmann's *Theology of Hope.*

The casual reader received the impression that theological designers, like their counterparts in the clothing industry, have the job of offering new accents, within limitations of materials and form, to sustain the interest of their clientele. Available to the theological designer are despair, paradox, *Heilsgeschichte,* Word of God, I-Thou, confrontation, Biblical theology, and an almost unlimited variety of existentialisms. Picking and choosing among these and other possibilities, Moltmann was thought to have caught the mood of the time and to have come up with a formula that captured the industry's imagination. Hope. It was perfect; a meeting of felt need with abundant materials in the warehouse of Christian tradition.

The " death of God " rage clearly had been a freak fashion with no staying power. It was not unlike the master of *haute couture* who overreached himself in 1967 by bringing out the entirely transparent dress. If for no other reason than professional survival, it was clear that designers could not permit the naked female form to be fashion's last word. So the transparent dress gave way to the maxi suit and the death of God has been replaced by hope and the designers have a new lease on professional life.

This account may not do justice to the way theologians work, but it is uncomfortably close to the way their efforts are received by the popular constituency of the theological enterprise. Within this fashion scenario most Americans first heard of Wolfhart Pannenberg. According to the reports, Moltmann was said to have surfaced the Biblical theme of hope, insisting that eschatology is not one among the many doctrines of Christianity but that Christianity is essentially eschatology. With the translation of his book (published in German, 1964), the "theology of hope" or "theology of the future" entered the vocabulary of religiously literate Americans. There has been criticism of course. Some argue that it should be "theology of promise," thus putting the focus on God's initiative rather than on man's aspirations. But almost everyone agreed that something new and worthwhile had happened in religious thought.

Moltmann was not depicted as standing alone. The debt to Ernst Bloch, the Marxist philosopher known for his adamant insistence that death is *the* question confronting man, was generally acknowledged. Among Roman Catholic advocates of the theology of hope, Johann Baptist Metz, of Münster, was usually mentioned and there was at least a passing nod to Karl Rahner in his more historical moments. Then, and usually only then, Wolfhart Pannenberg was named.

Pannenberg was a mysterious figure in the background, according to most religious journalists. He was, some said, busy constructing the philosophical underpinnings for the theology of hope which, as presented by Moltmann, remained more or less another theme of Biblical theology. To be sure, already in 1965 Pannenberg was being celebrated by some American conservatives for his defense of the resurrection as historical event. The ardor of *Christianity Today* (and others) quickly cooled, however, when they began to suspect that Pannenberg had something in mind other than firming the foundations of fundamentalism. For a brief moment of American acclaim, nevertheless, Pannenberg was known as the theologian of the resurrection. The rest of his work was hidden. There were occasional rumors about a "Pannenberg circle" in Germany that represented some new wave of the future. For most American readers there was little else to go on.

A few Americans had gone behind the rumors. Robert L. Wilken, a Lutheran theologian teaching at Fordham University and a close friend of Pannenberg, wrote several pieces introducing him to Americans. Carl E. Braaten's *History and Hermeneutics* (The Westminster Press, 1966) was intended to make straight the American way for Pannenberg's work. The third volume in Harper's *New Frontiers in Theology* (1967) had a "focal essay" by Pannenberg with critical responses by James M. Robinson, William Hamilton, and John B. Cobb, Jr. Then, too, Pannenberg spent some time teaching in the United States. First at the University of Chicago, the spring term, 1963, and later, 1966–1967, at Harvard and at the School of Theology at Claremont, California. During his two periods of lecturing in America, he also spoke at other theological schools, but the impact was something short of overwhelming. In fact his talk on "The God of Israel" at a much-publicized Harvard colloquium on Jewish-Christian relations was generally judged to be disastrous. More on that later.

Pannenberg had published in America a few essays in *Una Sancta,* the *Journal of the American Academy of Religion,* and *dialog* (four of these essays comprise this volume). Not until *Jesus — God and Man* (The Westminster Press, 1968), a book which Peter C. Hodgson says "may prove to be the most important work in christology since the great studies by Dorner and Ritschl in the nineteenth century," did a major work by Pannenberg appear in English. At the time of this writing, the English translation of *Revelation as History* (The Macmillan Company), is in its final stages and more translations are on the way. The present volume of essays should help inform the American discussion of Pannenberg, which has been conducted largely without benefit of his own writings. The essays in this volume constitute the most succinct and lucid statement of Pannenberg's overall enterprise available in English to date.

"The theology of Wolfhart Pannenberg has opened a quite

new front in the theological scene on both sides of the Atlantic. A good many issues that theologians had widely assumed to be more or less settled have suddenly been brought to the fore," writes John Cobb. Philip Hefner, of the Lutheran School of Theology at Chicago, in one of the most incisive critiques of Pannenberg's work, writes, " The intellectual task that Pannenberg has set for himself is a monumental one, namely, to construct a fundamental system of thought in which the primary ontological principle is futurity." The suggestion of radicality in these statements is essential to understanding Pannenberg's ambitious, perhaps audacious, intention. In speaking of the future, Pannenberg is not merely accenting a neglected aspect of the Christian tradition, nor is he merely suggesting that the concept of the future should have priority in theological thought, although he would agree with both these contentions. His intention is more encompassing than that. He argues for a new way of understanding the structure of reality. For Pannenberg, Christian theology cannot be narrowly theological. Theology either illuminates the public understanding of human existence or it has no worthy claim on our attention. Pannenberg's effort can be ignored or challenged, but it cannot be appropriated superficially simply to enrich our religious language with new rhetoric about hope and openness to the future.

1

A " profile " of a theologian should focus on his research, writing, and thought processes rather than on the personal characteristics of the man. His theological production, of course, is refracted through the peculiar composite of experiences, hopes, and anxieties that make the man. It is particularly appropriate to Pannenberg's work, however, that we not be distracted by the kinds of personal considerations that play so large a part in much pietistic and existentialist thought. We must come to terms with the ideas, not necessarily with the pious self-consciousness of the theologian. Ideas are, to be sure, not autonomous; they are part of a more comprehensive history. Yet ideas have their own identity and are the currency of the intellectual enterprise. With this caution in mind, I venture a few personal remarks about Wolfhart Pannenberg.

We met in the fall of 1966 at Gettysburg, Pennsylvania, in the home of Robert Wilken, who was at that time teaching at the Lutheran seminary there. At first meeting, Pannenberg strikes one as being quite different from the stereotype of the German academic in appearance and manner. An unprepossessing man of average height and unathletic build, he has a remarkably youthful, almost boyish, face topped by abundant dark-brown wavy hair brushed far back on the head; a playful smile under a slightly too large nose combines with eyes of intensive curiosity to give an impression for which the best word is "winsome." His manner in unfamiliar social situations is one of unassuming expectancy. The voice is quiet and well modulated; his English, a precise combination of carefully selected vocabulary. Students who have gone to hear him have been known to express disappointment at their first impression; his presence is pleasant but hardly commanding. His platform style, if that is the term, is emphatically understated, betraying his assumption that people attend lectures to wrestle with ideas, not to be stirred emotionally.

Pannenberg is an engaging conversationalist and that first meeting extended itself to several days of intensive exchange on the otherwise tranquil lawns of the battlefields of Gettysburg. These exchanges were to continue during his stint at Harvard, through several weeks when the Pannenbergs were our houseguests here at St. John's in Brooklyn, and in a sustained way through extensive correspondence. I mention this to expose what may be the prejudice of this introductory essay. It is written by one who has been confirmed many times in his estimate of the rewards involved in learning from and disagreeing with the ideas of Wolfhart Pannenberg.

The Church of Saint John the Evangelist is a parish of the poor in a black and Puerto Rican section of Brooklyn. This was Pannenberg's first prolonged exposure to the other America, the America of the disinherited, and here one could see the empirical thrust of his thought as he related his ideas to particular experiences of social change and conflict. He and Hilke, his wife, struck up almost immediate friendships with some of the families of the parish and tried to enter into the hopes and anxieties of the black community. Such entrance, as everyone should know by now, is not easily achieved, yet the effort is significant. This and other experiences in America helped Pannenberg to rewrite extensively the last section of the third essay in this book, dealing with the ideas of justice and peace in democracy. At the time of his visit the focus of social protest in New York City was on the question of decentralization and community control of the schools. Pannenberg attended an especially lively hearing of the Board of Education in which several of our community organizations disrupted the proceedings in protest against the intransigence of the Board. Pannenberg expressed surprise at the rowdiness of the meeting and remarked that in Germany it would be a significant democratic advance if there was a structure such as a board of education even formally accountable to the community. His brief experience with the school question in New York City, however, provided an instance of the incongruence between formal structure, in this case of a demonstrably democratic intention, and social process. Such experiences inform Pannenberg's modestly precise definition, " Peace is a provisional state of justice that is mutually acknowledged by the several parties concerned."

A profile of Wolfhart Pannenberg must be largely an intellectual profile, for he is a relentlessly intellectual man. Yet his intellectual thrust toward the empirical makes necessary a lively exchange between experience and thought, an exchange that precludes dealing with ideas exclusively on their own terms, as it were. This unity of experience and thought is more than a personal intellectual style of Pannenberg's. It is, as we shall see, the result of a comprehensive idea of history that challenges the dichotomies of emotive over against intellectual existence, of discursive language over against the language of imagination. Pannenberg's theology argues for a continuity of events including the life of the mind. Ideas are shaped by experience, and experience is shaped by the ideas that are our equipment for reception and interpretation. In his writing and conversation, Pannenberg tends to understate the role of personal experience, holding himself primarily responsible to the ideas as such, both his own and those of others. This tendency must be attributed, not to a kind of arid intellectuality divorced from life context, but to his response to a theological situation in which psychological analyses and a preoccupation with the self-consciousness of the theologian have led to an obscuring of the theologian's contribution to the history of ideas.

It obscures nothing, however, to report that he was born in 1928, the son of a German civil servant; that he received the education usual for a gifted child of the solid middle class and early in life showed, as they say, promise of future academic distinction. Like almost all young Germans of that time, he participated in the doleful efforts to defend the *Vaterland* in the last desperate days of the Third Reich. As might be expected, his childhood memories of Nazism remain vivid and have had a great impact on his understanding of the precariousness of society in general and of the German people's determination for democracy in particular. He was not reared in a devout Christian home. James Robinson understates the fact when he writes, " Pannenberg's own road to Christianity had been more one of rational reflection than of Christian nurture or a conversion experience." It is in fact hard to imagine a more emphatically intellectual path to Christian affirmation than the one traveled by the young Pannenberg.

In 1950 Pannenberg went to Basel and came under the strong influence of Karl Barth. His subsequent polemic against Barth's position, a polemic that is usually hidden but frequently explicit, is clearly the disagreement of a man who continues to respect Barth's magisterial command of the theological tradition. Like Barth, Pannenberg intends to be a " Church theologian " who holds himself responsible to the continuing tradition of Christian reflection. Unlike Barth, Pannenberg believes the Church and her theology can only be understood as a part of the larger human community. This means theology is clearly subject to the canons of rationality that are operative in this larger community. There are obvious differences between Barth and Bultmann, but Pannenberg contends that they are similar in their surrender of the theological enterprise to a kind of arbitrariness and subjectivism. He argues against the ghettoizing of theology when faith is thought to be self-authenticating or when one subscribes to a closed and authoritarian notion of revelation. This, in Pannenberg's view, makes the Christian message only one among several world views that can be asserted, to be taken or left depending on individual disposition. The gospel must be convincingly argued from public evidence, says Pannenberg. Anything less is an abdication of intellectual responsibility that discredits the Church's mission in the world.

Pannenberg continued his studies in Heidelberg in 1951. Here were orthodox Lutheran theologians Peter Brunner and Edmund Schlink. Here also were Hans von Campenhausen and Gerhard von Rad. The last was then constructing his argument that in the writings of the Hebrew Bible theology is, in the final analysis, the interpretation of history. Here, too, Pannenberg continued his philosophical studies with Karl Löwith, building on his previous work with Nicolai Hartmann and Karl Jaspers. Here, finally, a circle was formed among a group of graduate students. This project in team theology, which later, and against his wishes, became identified with Pannenberg's name, included Rolf Rendtorff (Old Testament), Klaus Koch (Old Testament), Ulrich Wilckens (New Testament), Dietrich Rössler (New Testament and Practical), and, somewhat later, Trutz Rendtorff (Systematics) and Martin Elze (Church History). *Offenbarung als Geschichte*, published in 1961, was prepared over years of discussion and represents the result of the circle's teamwork as nothing else did or will.

While the position of *Offenbarung* was gradually emerging in the circle's discussions, Pannenberg had completed his doctor's degree in 1953 with a dissertation published in 1954 on *Die Prädestinationslehre des Duns Scotus*. He became *Dozent* at Heidelberg in 1955 after passing his *Habilitation* with a yet unpublished book on the history of the idea of an analogy between God and world from early Greek philosophy to Thomas Aquinas. He accepted a call to the church seminary (*Kirchliche Hochschule*) at Wuppertal as Professor of Systematic Theology and three years later, in 1961, took the same position at the University of Mainz. During the three years of his first lecture courses in Heidelberg he was focusing on the history of theology in the nineteenth century, and it was in this connection that he became more fully acquainted with and impressed by what he believes to be the true stature and hitherto unsurpassed intellectual achievement of Hegel's thought. In his lectures in Wuppertal, Pannenberg developed the main body of his anthropology and Christology. Since 1961, when he went to Mainz and *Offenbarung* was published, his production has been prolific, ranging from philosophical exercises such as the final essay of this volume to popular radio addresses on the role of religion in society. Since spring of 1968, Pannenberg has been Professor of Systematic Theology at the University of Munich.

With the work of Pannenberg and his associates, writes James Robinson, "a new school has been launched. This new movement . . . is the first to emerge from the German generation that was born well after World War I had passed, was raised in the throes of the Third Reich, World War II, and the collapse of 1945, and has reached maturity in the *Bundesrepublik*. It is also the first theological school to emerge in Germany within recent years that is not in one form or other a development of the dialectic theology of the twenties." Pannenberg's work has met with limited acclaim and vigorous opposition in Germany. One factor in its reception, not necessarily the chief factor, is the "generation gap" in German academia. Generation gap in Germany means something different from the way the phrase is used in America. It refers precisely to a missing generation, the generation swallowed up in what was also the academic disaster of National Socialism. There is no natural bridge between the twenties and thirties of Barth and Bultmann and the sixties of Pannenberg. Whether or not the sixties will be marked theologically by the emergence of Pannenberg is of course something to be revealed by the future.

Pannenberg's interests are wide-ranging and always intensive, as his ambitious theological effort demands. Politics, race relations, psychology, biology, and sociology all fall under his purview. Not, of course, that one can reasonably entertain the notion of being a "universal man" in the sense of achieving expertise in these several disciplines; but Pannenberg strives to test his theological constructs in exposure to many worlds of thought. His interest in art and architecture is particularly keen, as these are dimensions in which man has explicitly articulated his understanding of his universe. The Pannenbergs' manner of visiting a gallery is revealing. Preparations constitute

a model of thoroughness which should be emulated by only the
more hardy of travelers. There is extended research, followed
by strategy meetings and the procurement of equipment cov-
ering most every conceivable contingency. It is worthy of a
quartermaster's preparations for a major assault. The pace of
the excursion itself is breathlessly intensive, everything must be
seen and seen carefully. The merits of a painting are discussed
with reference to its historical context, the phase of the artist's
political development, and the history of its ownership.

Some of us visit an art gallery as a comfortable indulgence.
To Pannenberg it is an exhilarating task. After he finished at
Claremont, the Pannenbergs invited me to accompany them on
a tour of Indian civilization in Mexico. I pleaded other obligations that were real enough, but more likely declined because,
although I am several years younger than Pannenberg, I suspected I would not survive the rigors of the expedition. The
trip to Mexico and other excursions are more than energetic
tourism. Pannenberg had previously examined the ruins and
artifacts of the Mediterranean area and wanted to compare his
observations with the traces of man's self-consciousness in the
residual civilizations of the indigenous peoples of Mexico. This
interest in the developing phases of human consciousness is reflected in Pannenberg's yet untranslated *Was Ist der Mensch?*,
a brief book on anthropology. It is reflected also, for instance, in
the first essay of the present volume in which Pannenberg suggests that the idea of personality is derived from man's experience of God, rather than being an imposition on the deity of a
concept derived from exclusively interhuman experience. This
is the kind of question that occupies Pannenberg's attention on
occasions that might for others seem more casual. He is capable
of refined reflection on the nature of frivolity, but seldom is he
frivolous. He has keen insight into the meaning of abandonment, but seldom does he abandon himself in the sense of sus-
pending his faculties of critical reflection.

Pannenberg speaks and writes not for an audience but for a
companion. His is a dialogical existence in which the inner
cohesiveness that marks his own life-style is extended to his associations. If he does not suffer fools gladly, it is likely because
he takes other people's ideas more seriously than they do. He is

impatient and obviously saddened in the company of people who attach little significance to their own thought process, who, claiming openness to new ideas, casually reverse the thrust of their argument. He demands seriousness more than brilliance. How can a person claim to respect history if he does not respect the history of his own intellectual existence; or, as a practical man, to take "real life" seriously if he does not reflect on his experiences in an orderly fashion? The various postures of anti-intellectualism, especially among theologians, are no substitute for the intellectual life but simply a shoddy form of it.

Pannenberg, on the other hand, becomes so thoroughly engaged when he discovers the possibility of serious intellectual exchange that single conversations extend over several days. In the morning the remarks of the previous night are directly resumed with, "But I think you too easily equate the 'end time' with the end of time itself," or whatever was under discussion. And so through the day, with recess only for inescapable functions. Each nuance of a topic is explored and he reveals an unsuspected grasp of material on the most diverse subjects. It is not a brilliant performance on his part, for even a brilliant performance is still performance. Neither is it a game with arguments to be won and points scored. It is a driving determination to understand. Pannenberg has been criticized for what appears to be his intellectual arrogance. It is perhaps more accurate to describe it as his insistence that others come to terms with what he believes to be the distinctiveness of his viewpoint. In many ways he is a disarmingly modest person and ready to expose his arguments in vulnerability to other reasoning and evidence. Pannenberg's manner of argument, like his view of reality itself, is marked by an awareness of provisionality, an openness to a future that will alone prove or disprove our perceptions.

Provisionality in Pannenberg's thought is not a condition that excuses a lack of commitment. This is as true of the intellectual life as it is of commitment to social change. That is, we must have the maturity to recognize the tentative character of existence on the one hand and the urgency of embracing it as the only existence we have on the other. For many, not only for Christians, there is an unbreakable connection between commitment and certitude; we can only be thoroughly committed to what we are absolutely sure about. Christians frequently appeal to some authority, revelation perhaps, to establish the certitude of the premises on which they act. To Pannenberg's radically provisional view of existence it is objected that if we cannot know for sure, we cannot act with religious serious-ness. Pannenberg counters that religious faith is connected not so much to certitude as it is to venturing risk on the basis of reasonable probabilities. To be totally engaged in a provi-sionally perceived process is the style that explains both the seriousness and the modesty with which Pannenberg views his own thought. The Christological corollary to this is spelled out in the introduction to his *Jesus — God and Man* where he takes issue with Barth by arguing that Jesus has to be viewed " from below." Viewing Jesus or any other experience in history " from above " is simply not a live option for man in his provisional existence. Provisionality is a key term in understanding the per-sonal style and the work of Wolfhart Pannenberg.

Pannenberg argues for a unity of thought and action, seeing every event — whether it be a political or an intellectual event — under the larger rubric of history. His attempt to build a conceptual structure of reality is not opposed to the vital life-forces that some view as being antithetical to the intellectual process. How this is worked out personally may to some extent be deduced from the third essay in this volume, " The King-dom of God and the Foundation of Ethics." What Pannenberg writes on the nature of love, the relationship between lover and beloved in the face of the future, can be understood auto-biographically. Yet even here at the interstices of the closest personal relations there is no suspension of analytic faculties. Precisely at this point of most intensive personal communion our reflection should be engaged if, indeed, there is to be a genuine involvement of the whole person. That we frequently think of intellectual reflection as an intrusion in personal rela-tions, as being somehow hostile to such relations, is itself evi-dence of the fragmentation of man.

Man's internal fragmentation is a facet of the fragmented character of all our experience. The unity that Pannenberg affirms is a unity of the future. He does not attempt to create an artificial coherence by imposing a conceptual framework that ignores the diversity and pluralism in existence. Such an imposition of artificial unity is precisely the opposite of what the gospel of the coming Kingdom demands. Such an imposition would be an idolatrous attempt to freeze the provisional present and a denial of the true unity to be expected from the future. Yet even in the present we look for those evidences of the unity, or synthesis, promised by the future. In his search for these evidences, Pannenberg gives the impression of a brilliant but plodding detective retracing his steps again and again in search of new clues, not fearing to challenge the obvious and think the impossible. This methodical determination comes through in his writing. He eschews the rhetorical reaching for effect and disdains the glittering aside, inviting the reader to accompany him in going over the evidence piece by piece and considering what it may suggest. Those who read in snatches will find Pannenberg thoroughly unsatisfying. The reader should be prepared to enter into the process of his thought or not bother with Pannenberg at all, since he writes for a companion, not for an audience.

Whether Pannenberg's search and that of his readers is ultimately worth the effort will of course be determined only by the future. What Pannenberg is suggesting is that there is really no alternative to the search. More positively, we are urged to take ourselves seriously as events in man's intellectual history. If we do our work well, men three generations removed will have to come to terms with our effort. Our work is for that future and for the future beyond that. Thus the theologian should gladly sacrifice 100,000 readers now for ten serious readers a century from now. This does not mean the theologian can disdain the opinion of his contemporaries, for he is well aware that his thought is shaped in the literary and verbal forum of intensive cross-examination and debate. The theologian's historical consciousness about his work, however, liberates him from the compulsive need for immediate acceptance.

There is a certain givenness about the history of an idea. Our intellectual confidence, Pannenberg's work suggests, rests on our workmanlike effort to master that history. Concepts such as justice, love, freedom, and progress are intellectual stories. When, in the mind of even one person, that story interacts with what in Pannenberg's view is the genuine newness of the present, there is a historical event that has an effect upon the idea that must be taken seriously by subsequent thinkers. In this light, a theologian's historical consciousness about his vocation is neither arrogance nor overwrought ambition but a logical corollary of this understanding of the historical process. Pannenberg's overarching argument thus suggests a way in which the theological enterprise can regain its nerve by extricating itself from the trap of compulsive relevance.

This view of history is also suggestive for handling the polarities of radical and conservative that are evident in almost every area of contemporary life and thought. The type of radicality that places sole emphasis upon discontinuity, that views the future as the force standing in utter contradiction to past and present, is foreign to Pannenberg's thought. This distinguishes Pannenberg from the run-of-the-mind revolutionist and also from Jürgen Moltmann's eschatological picture in which the future is more or less discontinuous with past and present. The genuine and radical newness of the future is not weakened by the idea that the power of the future (a kind of code phrase for God) embraces to itself the past and present of which it is both the source and destiny. It is through the events of the past which have been released, as it were, by the future that we are able to anticipate the future at all. This is especially true of those events which have a highly " proleptic " character, that is, events that signal further realization of the future from which they are derived. This ontological or metaphysical premise is central not only to Pannenberg's argument but also to his understanding of the theological enterprise of which his argument is part. Pannenberg is not content to rearrange the furniture in the house but presses on to rediscover the shape of the house itself. He reports that it is a futuristic structure both in derivation and direction.

More important than the furniture are the inhabitants. I have spoken of the broad spectrum of Pannenberg's intellectual interests and the dialogical nature of his thought process. The theological vocation cannot be an individualistic exercise by a recluse secure in a private room. As there is a linear historical consciousness about human thought, so also there is a strong sense of the interdependence of contemporary minds. The much discussed Pannenberg " circle " is to be understood in this light. The communal milieu in which Pannenberg's thought has developed is not designed to support an in-groupishness or an intellectual club, nor is it supposed that there can be some superficial synthesis of intellectual disciplines. The " circle " is based upon the awareness of the social character of thought, or the sociology of knowledge. This awareness compels a certain modesty about one's own reflection; there can be no illusions of uniqueness, no individualistic presumption about the singularity of one's cerebral processes.

Pannenberg's thought on the sociology of knowledge has been influenced strongly by George Herbert Mead and, among more recent American writings, he is impressed by Peter L. Berger and Thomas Luckmann's *The Social Construction of Reality* (Doubleday & Company, Inc., 1966). Peter Berger has remarked that one of the first things that impressed him about Pannenberg is that when Pannenberg mentioned Mead he did not mean Margaret. Of course Pannenberg understands the sociology of knowledge in connection with futurity. Here as elsewhere his work cannot be understood if the reader loses sight of the ontological presupposition of the priority of the future. The " circle " and every other joint intellectual effort, as indeed every human association, is valuable to the extent that it anticipates the synthesis of the future, to the extent that it is a proleptic event. Although the " circle " as originally constituted has become less important in Pannenberg's work, the insights from which it was shaped continue to be operative in his theological vocation.

The notion of an ultimate synthesis in which the disparities of the present will be resolved is one of the points at which Hegel's influence is most pronounced. At the same time, the role in Pannenberg's thought played by Jesus' message of the imminent Kingdom is among the factors that preclude classifying Pannenberg simply as a neo-Hegelian, a classification some critics have too readily ventured. Similarly, the mistake has been made of classifying Pannenberg's futuristic view with

that of Teilhard de Chardin. There are, of course, some important points in common: the recognition of the radically provisional character of existence, the anticipation of human destiny fulfilled in the reality signaled by the Christ, for example.
But Pannenberg's understanding of the generic power of the
future itself decisively distinguishes him from the thoroughly
evolutionary and teleological view espoused by Teilhard and
others. The same caution must be exercised in associating
Pannenberg with Whitehead, to whom he readily acknowl-
edges his indebtedness. Readers familiar with Hegel and
Whitehead, these two in particular, will find no difficulty in
detecting their influences but will do well to remain alert to
Pannenberg's departures. His differences from his mentors
amount to much more than his appropriating their thought in
a more faithful adherence to the Christian tradition and an
emphasis on Jesus' gospel of the Kingdom thrown in for good
measure. Again, the fundamental difference, from which other
differences flow, is the ontological priority of the future.

Purity of heart, says Kierkegaard, is to will one thing. The
precise and erudite lines of Pannenberg's writing do not con-
ceal his passion to will the future. It is too much to say of any
living man that he has purity of heart, but it occurs to me to
say it of Pannenberg. Perhaps it is more accurate to say that
Pannenberg wills to discover the truth about the future. That
is something short of, but inextricably related to, willing the
future itself. In either case, the relation to Jesus' preeminent
imperative to "seek first the Kingdom" is not incidental. The
urgency and breathtaking scope of Pannenberg's intention I
find refreshing in a time when most theologians seem to be doing the theology of other men's theologies or pursuing narrowly
circumscribed "problems" or investigating "interesting questions." Pannenberg dares to declare that theology's task is to
seek the truth. As readers who have worked through the minu-
tiae of his Christology, for instance, will witness, Pannenberg
does not disdain the particulars in favor of the grandiose. But
his most technical labors are consciously related to the larger
task of illuminating, on the basis of public evidence, the truth
about the universe in which we find ourselves.

2

The truth about the universe, Christian theology contends, is that the Kingdom of God is at hand. Something new is about to happen, indeed is happening, and will one day have happened in its fullness. The fact that the something new is happening now precludes the posture of passively waiting for the future. It also means, as we have seen, that there is a purposive continuity in history. Pannenberg seldom speaks of the Kingdom of God without using the adjectives "coming" or "imminent." This is to make clear that the Kingdom is not simply "out there" somewhere in the future but is constantly releasing its power in the creation of the present moment. Carl Braaten prefers the phrase "oncoming Kingdom" to accentuate the sense of movement, and we might do well to follow his suggestion. Whatever words are preferred, Pannenberg's intention must be distinguished from any idea of the future that places the Kingdom as a static entity somewhere ahead of us, or from any suggestion that the generic power is moving from the past through the present to the Kingdom.

The coming Kingdom is the overarching reality that informs our understanding of existence. Pannenberg posits this in full awareness that ours is a time suspicious of overarching meanings and of the more ambitious explanations of reality attempted by older philosophies and theologies. Yeats voices the modern anxiety:

> Turning and turning in the widening gyre
> The falcon cannot hear the falconer;
> Things fall apart; the centre cannot hold;
>
> . . . .
> The best lack all conviction, while the worst
> Are full of passionate intensity.

In his essay on the Kingdom and Christian ethics, Pannenberg speaks to the frightening recognition that "the centre cannot hold." He surveys the history of man's struggle for a linchpin by which values can be secured and argues that there can be no securing center within existing reality. The power of the future alone makes all things cohere. Every effort to secure things as they are is sin, which is the unwillingness to entrust one's self to the future rule of God proclaimed by Jesus.

This future role of God, the imminent Kingdom, is the issue of life-or-death decision in the preaching of Jesus. Sin is not the transgression of immutable laws but the distrust or unbelief that results in building defenses against the future. Contrary to some popular "situational" ethicians, ethics does deal with an absolute, namely, the Kingdom of God. But the absolute is not yet available to us in its fullness, to have and to hold or to measure our behavior. Therefore Christian ethics is marked by tentativeness or provisionality, relativity if you will, not because there is no absolute but because the rule of God has not yet come in its entirety. Pannenberg suggests to us that ethics is properly based on the question of being, of ontology, rather than on imperatives. No imperative derived from existing reality can serve as the foundation of ethics. That means no authoritative statements from the past, no notions of the higher good or of "the loving thing to do," as these are derived from experience, can serve as the ethical foundation. In fact the best-intentioned effort to ground ethics in the past and thus to restrict the shape of the future is a miscarriage of the Christian gospel and must be judged as idolatry. The future is the foundation of ethics; any ethical system or religion that is structured so as to deny this reality, even implicitly, is contrary to the Christian understanding of God's purpose.

Pannenberg's grounding of ethics in ontology suggests a reconsideration of the "natural law" theme in Christian tradition. To be sure, any notion of natural law must avoid the implication of set patterns in a static universe, an implication that has contributed to the discrediting of the idea of natural law. Like the natural law concept, however, Pannenberg's thought suggests that the "oughtness" of human behavior is derived not from "this is what is commanded" or "this is what seems most worthy" but from "this is the way things are." "The way things are" is determined by the creative impingement of the power of the future, the oncoming Kingdom of God. Conversely, what is evil in "the way things are" is the consequence of man's hostility to the oncoming Kingdom.

Hostility to the future is reasonable if the future is more nightmare than dream, more enemy than friend. The good news in Jesus' gospel is that the future is not an entirely unknown quantity or anonymous force. The future is beneficent, the future is the Father who cares, it is the Father who is love. Love is the force of coherence, therefore the future is not in radical discontinuity with past and present but promises fulfillment to past and present. This insight is crucial to understanding the more explicitly political dimension of Christian ethics in Pannenberg's thought, and touches on current efforts toward a theology of revolution.

There is, of course, an element of discontinuity in history in that our present vision of the future is highly tentative and in that man has erected structures of hostility to the future. The future is genuinely new; it is not established by our projections, but reveals the surprises of God's initiative. To such structures of hostility, then, the future appears not as fulfillment but as the shattering wrath of God. These structures of hostility, it should be noted, seldom take the form of explicit enmity toward the future. To their creators and protectors they appear as structures of security. The burden of Jesus' parables is directed toward illuminating the hostile and self-defeating character of these structures of security, whether the structure be the full barn of grain or simply everything included under the term "mammon." To those who do not trust the promise of the future, the future is a threat. The power of the future, God, is not less loving to some than to others. His love is indeed universal, falling as the rain upon both wicked and righteous. To the wicked, however, the surprises of God's initiative appear as destructive of everything in which he has placed his trust.

There is then this discontinuity of partial vision and of judgment within the larger process of history. The conservative radicality suggested by Pannenberg's thought is implied in two characteristics of the future. We observe about the future that it is marked both by contingency and by unity. To contingency are related such characteristics as freedom, unboundedness, unexpectedness, discontinuity. To unity are related love, coherence, fulfillment, continuity. Conservative radicalism is not a middle way between extremes but a comprehensive response to the structure of reality itself. In Pannenberg's work, there is truly a *theo*-logy of social ethics. That is, the understanding of social change is clearly and inextricably connected to the doctrine of God, for everything that has been said about the power of the future is in fact said about the nature of God.

Pannenberg's personal attitude toward those of the political right and left who "are full of passionate intensity" is somewhat reserved. Both the right and the left tend toward erecting structures of hostility to the future, the right by securing itself against the future and the left by attempting to impose its revolutionary projections upon the future. The right denies the trustworthiness of the future (unity) and the left denies the initiative of the future (contingency). In the conventional political sense of the term, Pannenberg is more conservative than the structure of his thought would seem to warrant. In the German situation, however, especially in the German academic situation, he is considered something of a liberal activist. When the student revolutions of 1968 surfaced at Berkeley, Columbia, Paris, Madrid, Munich, and elsewhere, Pannenberg responded sympathetically. He takes a role in party politics and has been among those professors calling for accommodation with East Germany on a settlement of border lines and other disputed questions. He particularly sympathized with the students in their protest against the "emergency laws" enacted by the Bonn Government. Like them, he has profound misgivings about the German people's determination to hold to democratic directions and processes in times of national tension and he does not make light of the danger presented by the right-wing resurgence in some sectors of German politics.

Pannenberg is too much the rational man, however, to join uncritically in the choral rhetoric of revolution. It should also be said in fairness that European intellectuals tend to be less enamored than Americans with the novelty of Marxist thought, and are more ready to criticize the utterances of *avant-garde* American "revolutionists" as being pop Marxism. To one American who was considering graduate work on Marxism, Pannenberg gave the advice that he would be making an academic investment in the past. To many European thinkers, Marxist theory has simply "lost its intellectual interest." In

America, where committed Marxists are few and far between, where there is no significant Community Party, and where consideration of radical alternatives to the prevailing economic and political system has usually been proscribed, the greater excitement generated by Christian-Marxist dialogue is understandable.

At the same time, perhaps some of Pannenberg's cautions against revolutionary thought are too conditioned by the Marxist experience. In the United States and in Latin America, revolutionary rhetoric is hardly obeisant to the rigid projections of the future proclaimed by Marxist theory. The "passionate intensity" of the American new left, for instance, frequently seems to have an amorphous view of the future, or even no idea about the future at all. For some it seems enough to be passionately opposed to what is. Be that as it may, Christian activists of all varieties do well to heed Pannenberg's statement: "We should not be carried away into saying that the Church must always be revolutionary. The future of God's Kingdom, in its saving of this world, is related to this world in an assertive and positive manner. This means that, for the sake of the Kingdom of God, the Church must resist the temptation to disdain the social and cultural heritage. A disdain for, and wasting of, this heritage is usually connected with revolutionary movements. We should not be reckless with history."

The Church is restlessly eager for change not because she despises the past but precisely because she cherishes the heritage. That is, Christians should know that the heritage cannot be saved by attempting to conserve it in its present forms. The heritage can only be saved by further development of its human significance. A careful study of both the theoretical and applied aspects of Pannenberg's thought contains the answer to the common complaint that an emphasis on the future necessarily depreciates past and present. Impatience with the past is healthy if the past is used in a restrictive manner, inhibiting the celebration of the present. Indifference to the future is understandable if the future is seen as a vague configuration of possibilities out there ahead of us. But the Church needs to be reminded and needs to remind the world of the unsatisfactory and indeed intolerable nature of the present without a fulfilling

future. And if the future as fulfillment is to be realized, the possibilities already existent in the present must be nurtured. Finally, our understanding of both present and future is derived
from the experience that is now past. If we despise the past,
we are incapable of understanding the present or of anticipat-
ing the future. The proclamation of the Kingdom and its confirmation by the raising of Jesus from the dead are events of
the past that in proleptic power are also the promise of the future. This event is the chief paradigm of history.

A theology of revolution (or as some partisans prefer, a theology *for* revolution) must be set within a theology of history.
Thus the Church is able to witness to the coming Kingdom and
against every denial of that hope, whether the denial be by
absolutizing the present or by dictating the future. Pannenberg
is aware that it is not only by a false theology of history that
the Church betrays her mission to bear witness to the Kingdom. This witness is severely compromised, for instance, when
the Church succumbs to the false otherworldliness that invites
an aloofness from the sweaty and unsatisfactory particulars of
man's social situation. Similarly any bifurcation of God's work
in history, such as the orthodox Lutheran notion of the right-
hand and left-hand kingdoms of God, compromises the
Church's witness. The same criticism applies to too sharp distinctions between civil and spiritual, secular and sacred. Biblical theology's emphasis on *Heilsgeschichte*, salvation history
as distinguished from ordinary history, must be critically reexamined. Any notion of authority or revelation that is somehow exempt from the historical process is to be rejected. There
is only history, and the rule of God is promised in that history.
Everything man says about revelation, salvation, revolution,
God, the future — all is encompassed in that history which we
have experienced in part and which is being fulfilled in the
coming of the Kingdom. Our future is not above us in heaven or
running parallel to us in "salvation history"; our future is
ahead of us.

Social ethics understood within this view of history is not
without its problems. There is obviously a high degree of risk
in a life-style that recognizes every grounding of security other
than in total dependence upon the future as idolatrous illusion.

Every political commitment must be marked by Jesus' pre-eminent imperative, " Seek first the kingdom." Those who " seek first the kingdom " will never be entirely at home with any social program or ideology that is, of necessity, short of the Kingdom. This should not, however, lead to political passivity; it is a restless dynamic to sight and support those signs of the absolute future which present themselves in the provisional present.

The more serious risk is that we may mistake the signs. " Do not say, Lo here, or, Lo there!" is a warning against over-confidence about our ability to sight the coming of the Kingdom. What we see now as a Kingdom sign may be repudiated by the future. But it is ours to seek the sign of promise, to commit ourselves to its fulfillment, and then trust to him who is the power of the future to vindicate our effort where we have chosen rightly and to forgive us where we have chosen wrongly. This is one of the most exciting insights of Jesus' message, that forgiveness is possible with God because he is the power of the future with whom is genuine newness. He is the power of love, related to but not confined to the past. He is able to overcome the past. We have spoken before about the coming of the future as the wrath of God that shatters the world's structures of hostility. Yet the same reality that appears as the wrath of God is also God's forgiveness to those who repent of their error and are ready to walk anew in the paths of righteousness that are now opened. Because the power of the future is the power of love, we can dare to pray for the judgment of God. The psalmist's plea, " Judge me, O God! " is, on our lips, not a declaration of our righteousness but of confidence that the coming of the future, while it means the painful shattering of our treasured securities, is powerful to liberate us from the evil of the past, to vindicate the right of the past, and to realize our aspirations toward full humanity.

Ethical thought based on the idea of the Kingdom of God is not new, of course. There is a superficial similarity in the " theology of the Kingdom " that marked the American Social Gospel movement of a half century ago. The similarities are more verbal than substantive; nevertheless, this can result in confusion. An incident in March, 1967, illustrates the difficulty.

Pannenberg desired to meet Reinhold Niebuhr, a man whose career is a legend also in Germany where he is the best-known American theologian (Paul Tillich is considered a German Lutheran expatriate). Driving up to Niebuhr's splendid little apartment overlooking the Hudson River, Pannenberg considered what subject would best be discussed with Niebuhr. The answer seemed obvious: the idea of the Kingdom in Christian theology. It was Niebuhr who had led the attack on the social gospel movement with its idea of extending the Kingdom of God in the social order. Apparently Niebuhr had heard of Pannenberg's work but had not read him. In any case, Pannenberg's question, " Now, almost fifty years later, do you think the place of the Kingdom in Christian theology should be reconsidered? " met with an unambiguously negative response. " Social thought that begins with the Kingdom of God, or even emphasizes it very much, inevitably ends up with utopianism. We've been through this business of the Kingdom before." Niebuhr asserted that Walter Rauschenbusch, who had such a passionate commitment about the Kingdom, was also incorrigibly naïve. " I am almost grateful for the act of mercy that he died before seeing what the war [World War I] had done to the world. It would have broken his heart." Regarding America's war in Vietnam and other matters, there was solid agreement between Niebuhr and Pannenberg, but theologically the conversation was disappointing.

The meeting is of interest for several reasons. Here was a relatively young theologian just coming into his period of greatest influence conversing with an old man reflecting on a half century's career of almost unbelievable consequence. Another aspect is that, after decades of Americans' going to meet the theological greats in Germany, a German theologian receives an audience, so to speak, with an American. Such thoroughly American theologians as Herbert Richardson, of Harvard, who wrote *Toward an American Theology* (Harper & Row, Publishers, Inc., 1968), may see this as a favorable omen.

More important to the matter at hand is that the conversation with Niebuhr indicates one of the problems Pannenberg's work will have in America. The language of the Kingdom seems inseparably associated with the social gospel move-

ment. Already there is talk about a " new social gospel movement." The essays in this volume should clarify, at least with
reference to Pannenberg, the radically different meanings intended today by language about the Kingdom of God and the
social dimensions of the gospel. " In distinction from 19th century evolutionary optimism," Pannenberg writes, " the Kingdom of God must always remain the Kingdom *of God*. It is not
a construction undertaken by extending Christian virtue, it is
not simply the kingdom of better men."

3

The Harvard colloquium on Jewish-Christian relations in
October, 1966, presented another difficulty in Pannenberg's
communication with the American scene. His paper " The God
of Israel" opened the conference, and it is easy to understand
the misgivings and hopes of the Jewish participants confronted
by a young theologian from the " new " Germany. The dominant " presence " in any meeting of Jews and Christians is the
specter of anti-Semitic history, most painfully the memory of
Nazi Germany to which Jews refer simply as the Holocaust. In
Jewish-Christian conversations, the shibboleth to which Jews
are most sensitive is any treatment of the finality of Jesus that
implies conversion.

Pannenberg's paper was unexceptionable in terms of his own
thought about Jewish apocalyptic being the context within
which Jesus proclaimed the coming rule of the God of Israel.
Most Jewish participants responded to the talk with icy silence, some engaged him with heated argument. Since the purpose of the conference was to further Jewish-Christian understanding, and since this was the initial meeting of the conference, Pannenberg made no new friends among the Christian
participants either. One still encounters theologians who respond to the mention of Pannenberg with a remark about the
misfortune at the Harvard colloquium.

Rabbi Arthur Hertzberg is among those who think it was
largely an instance of insensitivity to the nuances of Jewish-
Christian dialogue that have developed in America over the last
several years. " It is hardly fair to expect a European theolo-

gian to be alert to the nontheological mines that clutter the
field of Jewish-Christian relations. Pannenberg has probably
never known any Jews, to say nothing of working with us theologically." For obscenely obvious reasons, Jewish-Christian
theological dialogue is not a German phenomenon. Previous
generations of Christian theologians would not and the present
generation cannot benefit from exchange with living Judaism.
The Harvard colloquium was an important incident in helping
Pannenberg appreciate the peculiar problems and promise of
the religious situation in America.

Because of Pannenberg's strong interest in the relationship
between Christianity and Judaism, the Harvard experience
hurt. The kindness of Hertzberg and others was helpful and
later conversation with Rabbi Abraham Heschel was greatly
appreciated. Abraham Joshua Heschel has a crowded, smoke-
filled, book-stacked, periodical-strewn office near the top of
Jewish Theological Seminary, 122d Street and Broadway in
New York City. There the hospitality of this remarkable son of
Abraham supplied Pannenberg with one of the more congenial
evenings of his American visit. Alternating between German
and English, he and Pannenberg discussed at length the common grounding of the Biblical traditions, Judaism and Christianity, in the hope of the coming rule of God. This is the kind
of exchange that, had it been available to Pannenberg in advance, might have precluded the misunderstanding at the
Harvard colloquium.

What is true of Pannenberg applies to most Christian theologians in their efforts, often irenic in intention, to come to terms
with Judaism. For too many Christians, the " Jewish " in Jewish-
Christian dialogue means the Old Testament. Even the term
" Old Testament " is offensive to Jews, suggesting as it does an
outdated and even abrogated covenant; the " Hebrew Bible " is
preferred to designate that Biblical literature prior to Christianity. Above all, Christian dialogue with Judaism must deal
with contemporary, living Judaism rather than with the often
stereotyped Judaism refracted through the prejudices of early
Christianity.

Pannenberg's thought, at least formally, is highly suggestive
for Jewish-Christian relations. Unfortunately and inadvert-

ently, his contribution has been obscured by the inability to develop his thought in sustained exchange with Jewish theologians. In *Jesus — God and Man,* there are regrettable statements, at least implicitly inaccurate, which almost equate Judaism with legalism. " The rejection of Jesus was inevitable for the Jew who was loyal to the law so long as he was not prepared to distinguish between the authority of the law and the authority of Israel's God." (P. 253.) The conditional " so long as " seems to suggest that those who were not able to make this distinction were not typical of Judaism. But at other points in his Christology it seems that this inability to distinguish between the authority of the law and the authority of God is the archetypal characteristic of Judaism.

> It was not only that Jews, even the leaders of the Jewish people, were shown . . . to have acted unjustly, but it was that the law itself consequently became invalid. This explains why the Jews took offense at Jesus' cross, that is, at the cross of him who had been raised by God (I Cor. 1:23), or conversely, offense at the resurrection of him who had been rejected in the name of the law as a blasphemer. *With this message the foundations of Jewish religion collapsed.* This point must be held fast even today in the discussion with Judaism. One may not be taken in by benevolent subsequent statements of liberal Jews about Jesus as a prophet or allow that the conspiracy for Jesus' death was merely a failure of the Jewish authorities. . . . The conflict with the law in the background of Jesus' collision with the authorities must remain apparent in all its sharpness: either Jesus had been a blasphemer or the law of the Jews — *and with it Judaism itself as a religion* — is done away with. (Pp. 254–255, emphasis added.)

This view of Judaism is highly objectionable and thoroughly disappointing in the light of the suggestiveness of Pannenberg's view of history. Is it not possible that there are several legitimate interpretations of the Hebrew Biblical tradition? One interpretation, for instance, was represented by the leading parties among Jesus' Jewish contemporaries, another by Jesus, and yet another by the early Church. The development of the last interpretation moved beyond the positive statement that Jesus was an event of fulfillment for the Jewish tradition to the negative assertions about the blindness, stubborness, and, finally, hostility to God which characterized the Jews. Largely from this last interpretation the world has reaped the whirlwind of anti-Semitism. In his Christology, Pannenberg argues that the resurrection definitively settled the interpretation of pre-Christian Judaism. If it is true that Jewish religion itself collapsed, then what is the Judaism of subsequent centuries and of our own day?

In more recent exchange Pannenberg says he agrees with Hans Joachim Schoeps, who writes in *The Jewish-Christian Argument* (Holt, Rinehart and Winston, Inc., 1963): "The messianism of Israel is directed toward that which is to come; the eschatology of the universal Gentile Church toward the return of Him who has come. Both are united by one common expectation, that the truth, which we do not know, which we can only guess, is *yet to come*, in that hour when the beginning is swallowed up in the end." At that time Jewish-Christian dialogue ends and the unnatural bifurcation of Biblical religion is resolved in the fulfillment of God's promise. This points to a new and more hopeful way in Jewish-Christian relations, a way that is dramatically in agreement with Pannenberg's understanding of the structure of reality. The goal of dialogue cannot be conversion in either direction, nor is unity to be achieved by negotiating differences. Rather are Christianity and Judaism both provisional forms that await the healing truth which is to come. Our unity is in our participating in a common history and in our common expectation regarding that history. Jesus, in whom the goal is signaled, is with us as a Jew in the community of those who share what is essentially a Jewish hope of the universal Kingdom.

We can look forward to Pannenberg's further work relating this view of Jewish-Christian relations to what he says in *Jesus — God and Man* about the finality of Jesus and its implications for Judaism.

The perceptive reader will have suspected by now that this discussion of Jewish-Christian relations is but one facet of a larger problem in Pannenberg's work: the particularity of Christian history and its claims for Jesus. Contemporary theology, notably in the Bultmannian tradition, is able to separate the "meaning" of Jesus from the historical event of Jesus. This is not possible for Pannenberg. The event of Jesus is not only the chief paradigm in the consciousness of the Christian believer but public evidence available in history and having a claim on reason's effort to conceive the structure of reality.

Pannenberg takes what may appear to be a hard-nosed attitude toward historical fact. History is not the clay to be shaped to fit contemporary world views or to accommodate religious needs. Ronald Gregor Smith represents a more currently popular approach: "Our basic question is not, What is the meaning of history? but, Is there any meaning in history at all? And the simple answer is: we cannot tell. But to this answer we must add, 'But we can give it a meaning.'" (*Secular Christianity;* Harper & Row, Publishers, Inc., 1966.) Pannenberg argues to the contrary that the "meaning" of history is to be derived from history, not imposed upon history.

To clarify Pannenberg's intention it is helpful to juxtapose a further statement by Smith which is itself typical of much contemporary theological thought: "It is clear from the debacle suffered by the liberal critical investigation that the time of the historical approach to the life of Jesus is past. It has proved to be a cul-de-sac. There is no way of reaching a picture of the facts which is objective in the sense of being unassailable, unproblematic, and generally accepted. And even if there were, *per impossibile,* such a general agreement, it would not be satisfactory. For the facts would have to include much more than has been regarded . . . as the factual source of Christian faith, if justice is to be done to that faith itself." (P. 80.) The assumptions reflected in this statement are among the questions which, as John Cobb wrote, contemporary theology considered closed and which Pannenberg has reopened. Pannenberg's concern is not to give a meaning to history that will "do justice to the faith" but to see whether the faith is justified by history.

Pannenberg has no illusions about being able to reach "a picture of the facts" that is "unassailable and unproblematic." He has written at length on the interpretation of history and is fully aware that the interpreting factor is itself part of the historical process. But we must make do with what we have, and what we have is history. The results of historical study remain eminently "assailable and problematic." The final truth is revealed only in the *eschaton,* and, while we may find knowledge short of the Kingdom to be somewhat unsatisfactory, there is no excuse for positing some kind of "faith" or set of "meanings" to which we would conform the experiences of history. If we would seek the truth of history, we cannot demand that history bear our truths.

The particularity of the Christian tradition and its claims about Jesus cannot honestly be accommodated for reasons of ecumenical strategy. The claims of the tradition must be constantly reexamined on their own merits, as it were, and the implications must be drawn without compromise. At the same time, the very problematic and assailable nature of our findings should induce the intellectual humility that is essential to true ecumenism, whether that ecumenism be in relation to Judaism, to other religions, or to the secular mind. We shall return to some of these issues in connection with Pannenberg's understanding of "theology of reason." Meanwhile something should be said about the significance of Pannenberg's thought for the Church's preaching and piety.

4

Pannenberg is a "Church theologian." He holds himself responsible to, although not restricted by, the Christian tradition and participates in the teaching and sacramental life of the Christian community. In a time when it cannot be taken for granted that theologians pray, either privately or in the community's Eucharist, Pannenberg is a Church theologian. As the second essay in this volume reveals, Pannenberg's theology assumes that Christianity is not merely a bundle of interesting ideas but is a corporate venture with a piety and life-style appropriate to the expectation of the coming Kingdom. In theology there should be no gap between the classroom podium and the congregation's pulpit. Of course there is a difference in theological manner and to some degree in purpose, but the central thrust in both situations is to explore the truth of the gospel of the Kingdom and its implications for thought and behavior. To be sure, the pulpit is situated in the larger context of cultic remembrance, celebration, and the edifying of the community for specific service. The whole of the community's life both informs theology and is informed by theology. Theology is not imposed upon the Christian community from above but is nurtured by the community that sustains the memory of Jesus and the tradition of thought that has accompanied that memory. It would be the very opposite of Pannenberg's position to infer from this that theology is an ingroup Christian enterprise. Christian theology, while it finds its place within the whole of human thought, is specifically related to that identifiable community called the Church, a community that lives in explicit intentional response to the gospel of the Kingdom.

As a parish pastor engaged in the sublime absurdity of preaching, I have been impressed by the way Pannenberg's theology can inform and enliven the teaching ministry of the Church. Earlier we looked at ideas such as judgment and the wrath of God and their renewed significance in view of Pannenberg's argument for the power of the future. In a similar way we consider two problems that present conceptual difficulties in the worshiping congregation, briefly noting the way in which Pannenberg's approach might be applied: the problem of the connection between Christian identity and involvement in social change and the problem of the discrepancy between what the Church says about herself and what she experiences herself to be.

Conventional Christian piety, especially of the Reformation traditions, suggests that we should love our neighbor, support the struggle for racial justice, work for peace, and generally be socially responsible. The rationale for such activity is usually presented in terms of responding to the forgiving love of God. Everyone who cares for a congregation knows how often this exhortation falls flat. There is what might be called a gratitude gap; people simply do not feel the response of gratitude or whatever it is that is supposed to impel Christian love. It is not that they do not believe it in the usual sense of that term. In fact we discover that those who seem to accept the forgiveness of God as an unquestionable certitude and who indeed are terribly glad to "be saved" are often least disposed toward social involvement.

In conventional piety there is no *necessary* relationship between Christian existence and ethics. If I am now loved by God, forgiven by God, and thoroughly established as his child in the community of the redeemed, then love for my neighbor may be an appropriate response, it may be the decent thing to do, but it is not a constitutive part of my being Christian. Such piety assumes a past-present, cause-effect relationship. The breakdown between cause and effect, between past forgiveness and present ethics, cannot be repaired by saying, "*If* you do this and refrain from doing that, then you will be forgiven." That way lies the most blatant works righteousness.

Conventional piety is stranded on the static scenario of some kind of negotiation between man in his present existence and God in his. Pannenberg suggests that God's existence and his rule cannot be separated. The gospel is that God is coming into his rule and, therefore, in an important sense, is coming into existence, into existing reality. To have life, then, is to anticipate this future. The thrust of devotion is not from natural to supernatural or from human to divine, but in reaching out to welcome the future of God's promise. The dynamic of Christian piety is the yearning for what is to be, not gratitude for past forgiveness. There have been experiences of forgiveness, as well as other events for which we are grateful, in the past; the religious significance of these is that they stimulate our yearning for the future of which they were signs, but a future that is still ahead of us. This piety is not an amorphous longing, but is communion with that specific event which most clearly signaled the future, Jesus the Christ. In communion with Jesus, a communion that is cooperation with his continuing ministry to the world, we have a foretaste of the final fulfillment.

Jesus is the moment in our common history in which destiny was completely anticipated in a personal event. He is the archetype of the proleptic event in whom the "end time" participated in our time. The chief evidence of this is his being raised from the dead to new life. Death is the inescapable evidence of the provisional and unsatisfactory character of our existence; it is the master negator of all our striving for a better world. The gospel is that death is not the last word; the liberation of the world is promised and all who live now by that promise will be vindicated by the future.

It is not enough to be relevant or to get with the action. The kind of Christian engagement in social change that has staying power because it is rooted in Christian piety is that of the martyred Martin Luther King: "I have seen the promised land. I may not get there with you. But it doesn't matter now. We as a people will get to the promised land. My eyes have seen the glory of the coming of the Lord!" Whether this is more than heightened rhetoric depends upon the truth of the gospel. Resounding through Pannenberg's theology is the Pauline thesis, "If Christ is not risen, our faith is in vain."

The second illustration deals with how the Church understands herself. It is a mark of honesty that many preachers confess to being unable to use the metaphors of Biblical language to describe the Church as they know her: body of Christ, people of God, a holy people, *et al.* We can say these are simply poetic phrases, but why use them if they have no referent in reality? We can escape into talk about an "invisible Church" composed of true believers to whom these Biblical descriptions apply. We can choose the simplistic verbal solution of *simul iustus et peccator* (at the same time righteous and sinner) that dismisses the discrepancy between what the Church empirically is and what she claims to be as a "paradox."

Pannenberg's approach suggests that the Biblical language should be used and that to use it requires no compromise of honesty or sacrifice of intellect. Sociology need not be sacrificed to theology. The intention of the Biblical language is an intention of hope premised upon the coming Kingdom. To say I am justified or that this congregation is a community of the redeemed is not necessarily an exercise in false-consciousness, to use a helpful Marxist term. It is rather a statement about the destiny for which there is reason to hope, for myself, for the

Church, and for mankind. But does this language of hope have any bearing on my present self as I am, on the Church and the world as they are *now?* Yes, in two ways.

First, as mentioned before, we even now anticipate the future through sharing in proleptic or "preview" events. Therefore the apparently unsupportable and extravagant statements we make about the Christian life are descriptive of the actual situation to the degree that we anticipate the future of God's purpose, recognizing that this anticipation is always partial and provisional. Second, the Biblical language about the Christian life is true in the sense that what something *is* now must be perceived in terms of what it *is to be*. The meaning of a historical epoch is perceived in retrospect. The meaning of a human life and, likewise, the meaning of the whole of history will only be revealed in the completed rule of God. When the meaning of something is finally revealed, however, it is obvious that that is what it always was. In this sense also, the future determines the present.

This second point is crucial. When we speak of the future of something, we are speaking not only about what that something will be but about what that something already is. The truth of the matter can be seen only at the end of the matter. The language about the Church, then, is a language from the perspective of the future. The same reasoning is apparent in Pannenberg's Christology, to cite another example. That is, it is only in view of what happened to Jesus in the resurrection that we can look back on his preceding life and apply the statement, "Jesus is God," to the whole event of Jesus of Nazareth.

The Biblical statements about the Church, and about the world for that matter, are either false or nonsense, unless they are understood as statements of a future hope anticipated in the present. All of this might be caricatured as a grand evasion. The charge has in fact been heard that the "theology of the future" simply postpones to the future all the pressing questions that afflict belief in our day. It is a serious indictment. The language of hope is clearly not self-authenticating, it is not self-evidently true. It proves nothing to pick up this particular Biblical theme, hope, and with it try to infuse new life into the decaying corpse of Christian confidence. The answer to the indictment depends upon the rationality of the hope. "Be prepared," I Peter says, "to give a reason for the hope that is within you." In the next and final section we will see that the whole of Pannenberg's theology of the coming Kingdom can be understood in terms of that admonition.

5

Pannenberg's magnum opus is the theology of reason. There is no one book by that title, although there might be in the future, but theology of reason is the overarching theme of all Pannenberg's work. His commitment to rationality may well be one of the chief obstacles to the acceptance of his work in the current intellectual scene. As one radical seminarian declared, "We have to wage an all-out war against the Establishment, against systems, against warfare, against logic, against everything that stops us from being human." This demonology is generally acceptable, but we should think several times before including logic. In a time when pharmaceutical mysticism, revolutionary rhetoric, and the "happening" are high on the agenda of "reality experience," hard-nosed logic and relentless rationality should be valued as more than remnants from a more orderly past. As for theological work as such, we have been told for some time now that Barth and Tillich were the last of the great system makers. In this light Pannenberg's enterprise is distinctly unfashionable.

A theology of reason seems to many to be impossible or frightening or both. No doubt there is an element of personal disposition involved. Not everyone agrees that the mind is the crown of man who is, presumably, the crown of creation. Not everyone at some point in his life thrilled to the exquisite mental processes of Aquinas or Kant or Schleiermacher. What to one person is the aesthetic of rationality is to another a futile effort to capture the warmth of life in cold propositions. What to one is the supreme liturgy of reason offered in search of the truth is to another a blasphemous assault on the mystery of existence. It is true that after his mystical vision Aquinas declared all his magnificently reasoned writings to be as straw.

Those who claim similar visions may be warranted to concur in the judgment.

Luther, too, can be recruited in opposition to a theology of reason, condemning reason as a whore. For Luther, however, there remained the alternative of submission to the Word of God, a devout sacrifice of intellect to that Word which stands in judgment over reason. This option is no longer available to post-Enlightenment man — that there are many pre-Enlightenment people still around does not change the fact. The exclusion of this option is central to Pannenberg's position. There is no Archimedian point from which the rest of reality can be "objectively" viewed. There is no available revelation in the sense that history can be viewed from outside history, or from which we can view reality with "the eyes of God." We have only the eyes of men, within the limitations of our human condition, within the unfolding process of history. If we speak of the absolute and of God, and of course Pannenberg does speak in this way, it is because we have discovered evidence "from below" that compels such speech.

Theology of reason, according to Pannenberg, is something quite different from the arid rationalisms of the past. It is certainly not the rationalism of Lutheran, Calvinist, or Thomistic orthodoxy that attempted to organize revealed data in airtight conceptual compartments. Just as clearly, it is not the rationalism of reductive naturalism and of logical positivism, with their distorting type of abstraction that set the scene for earlier conflicts between science and religion. Nor is it the rationalism of some excessively abstract forms of idealism that seemed to concentrate on the thinking subject at the expense of the "life objects" of reality. As we have seen, Pannenberg's thought can be described as a highly personal and historical idealism in conscious debt to the work of Hegel. In contrast to the abstraction of naturalism, positivism, and idealism, some philosophers would posit pragmatism and existentialism as the "philosophies of life, action, existence" (John Macquarrie, *Contemporary Religious Thinkers*, p. 189; Harper & Row, Publishers, Inc., 1968). Pannenberg's argument challenges this distinction. Indeed he contests the fundamental subject-object antithesis as presented by Kant and in the various modifications that have continued to preoccupy philosophers. This is the philosophical foundation of what was earlier described as the unity of discursive and imaginative reason in Pannenberg's thought. The last essay in this volume gives some indication of the way in which Pannenberg handles the classic subject-object problem in terms of history and the future.

Theology of reason poses no threat to Christian piety. To be reasonable means to be open to those aspects of reality which do not conform to our conceptual processes. An adequate rationality takes into account the nonrational and what presents itself as irrational. Theology of reason does not try to flatten out the rough terrain of reality or to minimize the diverse and contradictory character of experience. There is no effort to impose a superficial synthesis. A reasonable man, says Pannenberg, stands in fearful awe before the mystery of existence, before the power of the future that will in its coming resolve the contradictions of experience. The beginning of wisdom is indeed the fear of God.

A sense of mystery is consonant with our reason and no substitute for rationality or excuse for mental laziness. If by reason one means the ideas that inform conventional wisdom, then there is much in the Biblical message that is " irrational." Jesus says the first will be last and the last first, he who loses his life will save it, and teachings of similarly unreasonable appearance. Paul asserts that he is a fool for Christ. Such statements, Pannenberg insists, do not constitute an abandonment of reason. To the contrary, Paul's precise argument is that his opponents are reasoning from false premises, by which premises he might be judged a fool. Against these he sets other premises and then proceeds to argue the case for the rationality of his position. Likewise, Jesus called men to follow him because his style of life is reasonable, if you will, given the premise of the coming Kingdom. If the most fundamental truth about existence is the imminence of the rule of God, from which all reality is derived and to which all hopes point, then it is perfectly reasonable that the thing to do is to commit oneself totally to the coming Kingdom. He who tries to save his life by holding back from trusting the future that Jesus proclaims will surely lose his life. This is the eminent rationality of discipleship. Of course, everything depends upon whether Jesus was right or not about the coming of the Kingdom.

That Jesus was right is not a foregone conclusion. He apparently was wrong about the timing of the Kingdom's arrival. According to Pannenberg, this does not mean his message was wrong. The proclamation of the coming Kingdom does not depend upon eschatological deadlines. The Christian message is that everything exists from the future of the God of love. In a way appropriate to his thought world of Jewish apocalyptic, Jesus' message was a statement about the structure of reality, an ontological statement. The question remains, Doesn't Pannenberg's argument leave open the possibility that Jesus may have been fundamentally wrong? Is it not possible that the very foundation of Christian hope may be mistaken? Is it not theoretically possible, at least, that further evidence will persuasively demonstrate, to cite the most crucial instance, that the resurrection accounts are a hoax? The answer must be yes. Pannenberg brings together the evidence that he thinks supports a very high degree of probability for the truth of Jesus' message. This is what historical study and reason can provide, a high degree of probability.

There is no absolute certitude, no irrefutable proof. Only the future will confirm the message of the Kingdom by the coming of the Kingdom, just as Jesus' self-understanding was confirmed by his being raised from the dead. Faith is not the ingredient that, when added to reason, provides certitude. Faith is rather the entrusting of ourselves to that power of the future which we are persuaded is trustworthy. Faith is not reason's backstop. Christians are not candid about the claimed rationality of their commitment, nor have they measured the risk of faith if the possibility of error is not left open.

In spite of previous denials, this approach may seem narrowly rationalistic. Pannenberg is well aware that the Christian life does not consist in a perpetual calculation of the evidences favoring Jesus' claims. Pascal wrote about the metaphysical proofs of the existence of God, " Even if they did help some people, the effect would only last for a few moments while they were actually observing the demonstration, but an hour later they would be afraid that they had made a mistake."

(*Pensées*, p. 212; Harper & Row, Publishers, Inc., 1962.) This is no basis for a vital religious life.

The "reason for the hope that is in us" is not, in Pannenberg's thought, a delicately balanced series of esoteric reasonings leading to a probable yet tentative conclusion about the nature of reality. The hope of the coming Kingdom is a lively and full-orbed Christian confidence supported by life experience, empowered by the Spirit of God, and expressed in the doxology of service. The Christian life is communion with the risen Lord, fellowship in the community of hope, celebration now of the Eucharistic banquet which is a type of the Kingdom feast of fulfillment. Yet this Christian life is not self-authenticating. No aspect of Christian existence can be exempted from critical reflection. Faith, even at its most fervent pitch, cannot substitute for the *reason* for the hope that is in us. Faith is not another kind of sight. Faith is daring to act in full awareness of the partiality of sight.

An incident illustrates Pannenberg's understanding of the role of reason in religious piety. Abraham Heschel was one day deploring much of what passed for liturgical reform. "These people want to take the mystery and the poetry from Biblical religion. They flatten out everything: no peaks, no valleys, no nothing. It's banal. They say that the old words cannot express what they mean. What arrogance! As though we had big new meanings for which the words of the Bible are not adequate. The truth is that the liturgy says ever so much more than we mean. That's what liturgy is for. We poor souls should aspire to the meaning of the words we say." I later repeated Heschel's words to Pannenberg when I thought Pannenberg was being excessively exacting in his theological criticism of a particular liturgical practice at St. John's. "Ah, yes," Pannenberg answered, "Heschel is right, the liturgy does say more than we can mean, and that is good. But we must take care so that in liturgy we do not say what we do *not* mean!" It is as though Pannenberg is arguing that reason is a full-fledged member in the Christian household. It is not just a hired guide to get us to the house, nor is it merely a guard to protect us when we are away. Reason must be a participant in the whole of the Church's life, even at the point of highest emotive abandonment, at the point of worship.

It might be easier for Pannenberg if he did not have this thing about seeking the truth with just quite this degree of intensity. Deep down in most of us who were nurtured in devout Christian homes is, I suspect, some slight nostalgia for a simpler, less complicated faith. We know we can't go home again. There are, nevertheless, the quiet nights alone when we whisper: " Now I lay me down to sleep. I pray thee, Lord, my soul to keep . . ." and for a brief moment we are again children secure in a faith unmolested by critical reason. I wonder how much of today's talk about the " crisis of belief " is a more sophisticated version of our anguished lament at the repeated discovery that we can't go home again.

This is not Pannenberg's problem. He was not taught as a child to believe that reason is the enemy of faith or that doubt is a disease to be exorcised by prayer or that submission to religious authority is a virtue to be cultivated. He came along in the style that " worldly Christians " favor as the description of modern man: pragmatic, skeptical, secular. He came inquiring of theology because he was a thoughtful young man with the kinds of questions about which theology presumed to speak: life, death, destiny, the purposiveness of the universe. He was not persuaded by theologians who asked him to compromise or abandon reason. Critical reflection was as reliable a friend as he had, and, having brought him to this point, he was not about to forsake it now. He suspected, however, that the Christian viewpoint might be more reasonable than its experts allowed. Perhaps through some failure of intellectual nerve they found it necessary to seek sanctuary in the fortress of specialized language and subjective experience surrounded by the moat of revealed knowledge.

Pannenberg's suspicion that the gospel might be reasonably presented is, of course, not foreign to the Christian tradition. In the third century, Gregory Thaumaturgus, a student of Origen, wrote to his teacher: " I should like to see you use all the resources of your mind on Christianity and make that your ultimate object. I hope that to that end you will take from Greek philosophy everything capable of serving as an introduction to Christianity and from geometry and astronomy all ideas useful in expounding the Hebrews' scriptures; so that what . . . philosophers say of geometry, music, grammar, rhetoric and astronomy — that they assist philosophy — we too may be able to say of philosophy itself in relation to Christianity." (*Una Sancta*, Vol. 24, No. 2, p. 35.) Origen's credentials have been under something of a shadow during much of Christian history, but today scholars are beginning to rehabilitate his reputation, and his example is pertinent to Pannenberg's effort. Origen is not the only example by any means, neither is Pannenberg Origen, nor is the twentieth century to be confused with the third. Like Origen and others of the church fathers, however, Pannenberg is prepared to submit Christianity's claims to the canons of reason and intelligibility by which other claims are tested. The need for such a testing is urgent in a time when theology's methods are considered as obscure by modern men as Christianity was considered irrational by the students of Hellenistic philosophy.

A theology of reason *can* only be undertaken seriously by one who is on friendly terms with man's rationality and *would* only be undertaken by one who cares about the missionary dimension of Christianity. Pannenberg hesitates to use the term " mission " because of its associations with intellectual imperialism. Yet mission is involved when one speaks of the public character of the evidence supporting Christianity's claims. If the gospel of Jesus is true in any significant sense of that word, it is true for all men. It is not an arbitrary viewpoint to be taken or ignored depending on whether one has a taste for that sort of thing. It does not say something " meaningful " only to those of sophisticated religious sensibilities. It has a claim on the attention of all men because it claims to describe the universe in which all are involved. Pannenberg is an apologist in a great Christian tradition. His is a difficult vocation. Outside the Church there is well-founded skepticism that a serious case can be made for Christian claims. Inside the Church there are myriad misgivings about the desirability of a theology of reason. It seems likely that the second obstacle may be more intractable than the first, for reason is the only available instrument to persuade those who are opposed to a theology of reason.

Wolfhart Pannenberg is a modern man and a rational man before he is a Christian man. Faith and reason, belief and experience, Christian commitment and modernity are not antinomies to be held in tension. He contends that he is a Christian because he is a modern and rational man. He presents the case with lucidity and intellectual courage. It demands examination and response.

RICHARD JOHN NEUHAUS

Brooklyn, New York
Day of Saint Matthew
September 21, 1968

Chapter I

Theology and the Kingdom of God

The message of Jesus centered in the proclamation of the imminent Kingdom of God. His word to those who were burdened with anxiety about food and clothing is representative of this clear focus, "Instead, seek his kingdom and these things shall be yours as well" (Luke 12:31). There is a striking difference, however, between the preaching of Jesus and the place that the Kingdom of God occupies in contemporary theology. Gerhard Gloege wrote some years ago, "Generally speaking contemporary Protestant theology in all its fields has lost the basic idea of Jesus' preaching." This loss is more recent than we might imagine. The Kingdom of God was a central motif in American theological history, notably from the Puritan divines to the social gospel movement. And in German theology, from Kant and Schleiermacher through Richard Rothe and Ritschl, there was no disputing the centrality of the Kingdom to the Christian message.

But the dogmatics of recent decades is marked by a steady erosion of the notion of the Kingdom of God. This erosion is usually explained by the conventional understanding of the Kingdom of God having been deprived of its exegetical foundations. From Kant to Ritschl and the religious socialists, the Kingdom of God and its propagation were goals to be achieved through man's labor. Today such thinking is dismissed as being simplistic or even dangerously naïve. But theologians of the past correctly asserted that where men comply with the will of God, there is the Kingdom of God. Taking this a step farther, they asserted that to extend the sphere of obedience to God's will means the extension and establishment of his Kingdom.

This assumption was upset by Johannes Weiss toward the end of the nineteenth century. He discovered that, according to the New Testament and to Jesus' message, the Kingdom of God will be established not by men but by God alone. The coming of the Kingdom will involve cosmic revolutions and change far beyond anything conceivable as a consequence of man's progressive labor. God will establish his Kingdom unilaterally. Therefore Jesus, and John the Baptizer before him, only *announced* the Kingdom of God, exposing every present condition under the light of the imminent future. This future is expected to come in a marvelous way from God himself; it is not simply the development of human history or the achievement of God-fearing men.

Digesting the Change

Theology today has yet to digest this radical change from the ethical to the eschatological understanding of the Kingdom of God. It is instructive to note how Johannes Weiss, Albert Schweitzer, and other New Testament scholars of their time, began to regard Jesus with a sense of estrangement. It is true that, in dialectical theology, eschatology became a slogan. But for Bultmann and for the young Barth, Jesus' eschatology is timeless and deprived of its temporal meaning. Dialectical theology disregarded Jesus' message about the Kingdom of God as an expectation regarding the concrete future. The intention of Jesus was an embarrassment, for it was all too obvious that his expectation of a cosmic revolution in the near future had been illusory. So theologians focused on Jesus' words about the presence of the Kingdom of God now. And where Jesus' words about the future have a clearly temporal meaning, these were modified by means of Christological or anthropological interpretations. No longer was the eschatological reality to be looked for in the future. It became fashionable to speak of the eschatological " deed of God " in Jesus himself and to declare his unique significance as an event opening new possibilities for human existence.

In the New Testament, however, Jesus' message of the imminent Kingdom of God precedes every Christology and every new qualification of human existence and thus becomes the foundation of both. Christological and anthropological interpretations cannot be imposed upon the preaching of the Kingdom, but must themselves be judged in the light of the Kingdom. This resounding motif of Jesus' message — the imminent Kingdom of God — must be recovered as a key to the whole of Christian theology. Not only is this recovery essential if we are to do historical justice to the notion of the Kingdom, but it also suggests more adequate approaches to the vexing problems in contemporary Christian thought. Two such problems are the notion of God — so widely discussed today — and an understanding of creation that is capable of coming to terms with the discoveries and projections of the natural sciences. This essay attends to these two problems. In future essays, I shall attempt to demonstrate the importance of understanding the imminent Kingdom of God for interpreting the Church and her relation to society and for discovering a new foundation for an ethics that will be able to cope with the relative character of traditional norms.

Futurity Is Fundamental

Our starting point then is the Kingdom of God understood as the eschatological future brought about by God himself. Only in the light of this future can we understand man and his history. God's rule is not simply in the future, leaving men to do nothing but wait quietly for its arrival. No, it is a mark of Jesus' proclamation of the Kingdom of God that future and present are inextricably interwoven. To understand this interrelation is one of the most problematic questions in contemporary study of Jesus' teaching. The accent of Jesus' message differed from the Jewish eschatological hope at precisely this point: Jesus underscored the *present impact* of the imminent future. Bultmann, Dodd, and others exaggerated the difference, however, to the degree of dismissing the futurity of the Kingdom of God in Jesus' message as a remnant of Jewish thought. In abstracting the present impact from the whole of Jesus' message of the Kingdom, the message was grievously distorted. Jesus indeed spoke of the presence of the Kingdom of God, but always in terms of the presence of God's *coming* Kingdom. Futurity is fundamental for Jesus' message.

The interweaving of future and present in Jesus' statements is not taken seriously by those who denigrate futurity as a hangover from Jewish apocalyptic. On the other hand, neither can we agree with Cullmann, who says that Jesus understood the Kingdom of God as beginning in his presence and only to be fulfilled in the future. It is more appropriate to reverse the connection between present and future, giving priority to the future. Of course this is strange for contemporary thought, but it corresponds to the fact that the starting point for Jesus' message was in the Jewish hope for the future Kingdom of God. Jesus' particular emphasis can be understood as a modification of the Jewish hope: God's Kingdom does not lie in the distant future but is imminent. Thus, the present is not independent from that future. Rather does the future have an imperative claim upon the present, alerting all men to the urgency and exclusiveness of seeking first the Kingdom of God. As this message is proclaimed and accepted, God's rule is present and we can even now glimpse his future glory. In this way we see the present as an effect of the future, in contrast to the conventional assumption that past and present are the cause of the future.

This priority of the eschatological future which determines our present demands a reversal also in our ontological conceptions. Let us see how this works out more precisely, beginning with the idea of God.

In Jesus' message everything is dominated by the idea of the imminent Kingdom of God. In Jewish tradition, the hope of God's coming Kingdom was more of an appendix to a piety shaped by the law given through Moses. With Jesus the eschatological hope itself became the only source of knowledge and guide for living. Whatever God demands from man and whatever he gives to man is comprehended in the message of the imminent Kingdom. Even the idea of God is affected by this message. Jesus did not develop the implications of his eschatological message for the idea of God any more than he developed a systematic interpretation of the law. As he restricted himself in the antitheses of the Sermon on the Mount to a criticism of particular regulations, so also he concentrated what he was saying about God in proclaiming the God of Israel as the God of fatherly love. Why he did not develop the idea of God more fully will become evident in connection with the peculiarity of Jesus' eschatological message. The point now is that Jesus did not spell out the implications of his message for our understanding of God's mode of being. Of course he might have done so if God's being were a point of controversy in the discussion he carried on with his opponents. But God's being was not an issue.

The situation changed somewhat with the meeting of Christian thought and Greek philosophy. However, the early Church did not feel sufficiently challenged at the point of its idea of God to warrant a reinterpretation of God's mode of being along the lines suggested by Jesus' message of the imminent Kingdom of God. The fact is that Christian theology accepted the philosophical notion that God rules as the highest spiritual being over the world, and thus failed to discover the implications of Jesus' message for the idea of God. In recent centuries, however, the conventional idea of God as the highest spiritual being has fallen into disrepute, and we are confronted with a new intellectual situation which not only warrants but demands rethinking our idea of God. In this task we would be foolish to ignore the undeveloped resources of Jesus' message for the Christian doctrine of God.

God's Being Is His Rule

We begin with the simple observation that God's being and existence cannot be conceived apart from his rule. Or, to put it in the language of the philosophy of religion, the being of the gods is their power. To believe in one god means to believe that one power dominates all. In explaining the first article of the Apostle's Creed, Luther says that only that god is the true one who can create heaven and earth. Only the god who proves himself master over all is true. This does not mean that God could not be God apart from the existence of finite beings, for God certainly can do without anyone or anything else. It does mean that, if there are finite beings, then to have power over them is intrinsic to God's nature. The deity of God is his rule.

Jesus proclaimed the rule of God as a reality belonging to the future. This is the coming Kingdom. The idea was not new, being a conventional aspect of Jewish expectation. What was new was Jesus' understanding that God's claim on the world is to be viewed exclusively in terms of his coming rule. Thus it is necessary to say that, in a restricted but important sense, God does not yet exist. Since his rule and his being are inseparable, God's being is still in the process of coming to be. Considering this, God should not be mistaken for an objectified being presently existing in its fullness. In this light, the current criticism directed against the traditional theistic idea of God is quite right. Obviously, if the mode of God's being is interlocked with the coming of his rule, we should not be surprised or embarrassed that God cannot be "found" somewhere in present reality.

The God of the coming rule is related to all that is finite and is the power determining the future of all that is present. The idea of the futurity of God is no mere subterfuge invented to evade the atheist criticism. We cannot save the well-known divine being simply by slipping it into a vague future because there is no room for it in the present. No, we must honestly question whether this idea of God, drawn from the message of his imminent Kingdom, has any validity for contemporary man and his understanding of reality. A positive answer depends on whether the extant world itself can be understood more adequately in terms of its being the expression of this power we call God.

Future Not Imprisoned

By conceiving of God as the power of the future, the word "God" acquires a new concreteness. When we say "power of the future" we should not limit ourselves to an arid or formal concept of future in contrast to the more real past and present. The future is not an empty category. This becomes evident when we inquire into how men actually experience their relation to the future. While it is true that the future can be foreseen and planned to some extent, man is constantly confronted by the future as by a dark and uncertain power threatening our lives or promising their fulfillment. For reasons which ought to be developed in a philosophy of natural science, I am persuaded that this experience of the ambiguity of the future is due not simply to our lacking full knowledge of the myriad particular conditions of the present. Rather, this experience of the future's ambiguity points to an essential indeterminateness or vagueness in the events of nature. In this connection we speak of the contingency of events according to which, in a particular instant, something is decided that was only a possibility before. This contingency does not make planning impossible by any means, but is a presupposition in all efforts to calculate the causes of events and to make them humanly purposeful. Humility is the better part of valor in the face of a future which is not the prisoner of past and present.

The Jewish and Christian idea of God is related to this element of contingency in nature and history. But what reason do we have for saying that it is God whom we confront in the contingency of events which, before they actually enter our world, share in the ambiguity of the future? What warrant do we have for saying that those contingent events are in fact acts of God from whose future they spring? At this point we have not yet estabished the assertion that God is the power of the future, but this much can be said: The contingency of events is a crucial presupposition for understanding the future as personal, and to speak of God is to speak of a personal power.

The Idea of Person

The notion of a personal God is attacked vigorously by atheists because it looks to them like an anthropomorphic projection of human personality in divine dimensions. Indeed, against that atheist suspicion, it is hardly possible to defend the notion of God's personality in terms of analogy to men. The notion of the personal character of God (and the very idea of God would be self-contradictory without it) can be asserted only if it is possible to eliminate anthropomorphic associations from the idea of the personal, or at least from the roots of the idea. The assumption that men first conceived of themselves as persons and then applied this conception to their gods is arbitrary and artificial. This assumption presupposes a secular self-understanding of man which is clearly an achievement of more recent history. It cannot be projected backward onto preliterate or archaic man. The reality of the gods was a primary datum of his experience, and he understood himself in the light of that experience.

Weighty evidence favors the idea of the personal having its origins in religious experience, in the encounter with divine reality. According to this view, the notion of the personal was later transferred to man because man was honored with a special relation to the gods. In this way the very possibility of anthropomorphic conceptions of the divine may be explained. Man's projecting of himself and his personality upon the gods presupposes a more basic idea of personality and is based upon man's encounter with the divine, while the particular characteristics of the divine personality are shaped by man's attributing his own particulars to the gods. The basic idea of divine personality seems to be related to man's experience of the contingency of events. There are enormous differences between the contemporary experience of reality and the experience of archaic man, but then and now only contingent events can be perceived as personal acts.

Contingency and Unity

There must be something more than contingency to justify understanding events as personal acts. Otherwise to speak of a contingent event may mean little more than to refer to the apparently erratic character of happenings. Contingency is not enough to give events a personal quality. The required additional factor is the identity of the power that is operative in a series of contingent events, a unity behind contingent self-expressions. This unity acquires identity by exhibiting some meaningful connection in the sequence of events. If this meaningful connection is understood in such a way as to replace the contingency of events with deterministic models of reality, the notion of a personal power behind those events is untenable. But so long as we acknowledge the genuine contingency of events, the basic precondition for personal encounter is provided.

Now it is time to ask if there is in fact a unity behind the contingent events that sprang from the future. The answer is already suggested in the image contained in the question. The power of the future can be conceived as being greater than any sum of individual contingent events. The future which confronts us is more than a number of finite events about to happen. The more ambiguous the future to which we look forward, the stronger is our impression of its lively indefiniteness, of its unpredictability. Because the future has not yet been decided upon, we attach to it the basic anxiety of existence. Human beings will never overcome this anxiety completely. Nor should we wish to be rid of this anxiety, for it is related intimately to something else which we attach to the future — hope for a more exuberant fulfillment of our existence. Anxiety and hope transcend the anticipation of single imminent events. Yet when events which we anticipated in anxiety and/or hope do occur, the ambiguity of the impending future congeals into finite and definite fact. In every event the infinite future separates itself from the finite events which until then had been hidden in this future but are now released into existence. The future lets go of itself to bring into being our present. And every new present is again confronted by a dark and mysterious future out of which certain relevant events will be released. Thus does the future determine the present. If we, in our anxiety and hope, contemplate this power of the future, we recognize both its breathtaking excitement and its invitation to trust. For those who accept the invitation, the world is widened with new possibilities for joy. In every present we confront the infinite future, and in welcoming the particular finite events which spring from that future, we anticipate the coming of God.

This entire argument presupposes, as we have seen, the concreteness of the power of the future. The future is neither empty category nor bundle of chances. It also presupposes that there is a single future for all events. To speak of the definitive unity of the world means that all events are moving ahead to meet, finally, a common future. In our experience, the existing connection of events and the fact of corporate unities direct us toward the unifying power of the future.

Three ideas are essential here: unity, the future, and sovereignty. Sovereignty establishes unity. The coming of God to his sovereignty over the world is his gift to the world, unifying its scattered events. The coming of God also means that God has the power over the future of those who are under his rule. Thus the circle is closed. Jesus' message of the Kingdom of God implies that the unity of the world is to be expected from its future. Therefore the unity of all things should not be understood in terms of an eternal cosmos but as something to be achieved by a process of reconciling previous schisms and contradictions. Reconciliation is a constitutive aspect of creation.

Unity is a subject of eternal interest to the philosopher. Unity is the most comprehensive characteristic of being, and medieval metaphysics counted unity among the transcendental marks of being. Everything is a unity to the extent it is at all. Unity is equally fundamental for gnoseology as for ontology, for knowing as for being. The drive to unity and synthesis permeates the dynamics of reason. We perceive things only as we discover unity in plurality. Everything that is, and everything conceivable, is by its very existence or conception "one." The quest for the ultimate unity which integrates and thus unifies everything is the question reaching for God, as that question has been asked since the beginning of Greek philosophy. For us, too, the way in which we must test any concept of God is by asking whether it can account for the unity of all reality. If an idea of God fails that test, it does not comprehend the power dominating everything and is, therefore, not a true concept of God.

Recognizing that unity and power belong together, we further note that the idea of power makes sense only in relation to a future. Only he who has a future is in possession of power. The notion of the Kingdom of God evokes a vision of the unity of each being and the unity of the whole world as flowing from the future. Far from creation being at one end of the time spectrum and eschatology at the other, creation and eschatology are partners in the formation of reality. The future decides the specific meaning, the essence, of everything by revealing what it really was and is. At present a being is "something," a unity in itself, only by anticipation of its unifying future. The future interprets the present and the past; all other interpretations are helpful only to the degree that they anticipate the future.

Summary

It is time to pause for a summary of what has been said so far. If the Kingdom of God and the mode of his existence (power and being) belong together, then the message of the coming Kingdom of God implies that God in his very being is the future of the world. All experience of the future is, at least indirectly, related to God himself. In this case every event in which the future becomes finitely present must be understood as a contingent act of God, who places that finite reality into being by distinguishing it from his own powerful future. Our existential awareness of the future provides evidence that our life is related to an abundant future which transcends all finite happenings. This power of the future manifests itself as a single power confronting all creatures alike. Thus this power may be properly conceived as the power unifying the world.

The Future Creates Past and Present

This conclusion leads to consequences which, at first sight, may seem even more strange than those exposed so far. If the future of all creatures is a universal one, that is, if each instance of reality has the same future, then the future to which I look forward today is the same future that confronted every earlier present. My future now was also Julius Caesar's future, the future of the prehistoric saurians and the future of the first physical processes approximately ten billion years ago. Thus I come to view past events as having eventuated from the same future to which I look forward. And, of course, those past events were the finite future of yet earlier events. The past is related in this way to the power of the future to which I look forward at present. Only in this way can I remember the past with gratitude or sorrow, knowing that past events did not occur as matters of inexorable fact but occurred contingently. And so we can now understand even our past as the creation of the coming God.

The unity of the future accounts for its power being already at work in the past. The superficial critic might suggest that the power of the future cannot reach back to the past and therefore is only a limited power. Were this the case, the Almighty God could not be identical with a power of the future as we

understand it from Jesus' proclamation of God's imminent Kingdom. But this difficulty is overcome if we recognize that God
has been the future of all past events. He gave the past a preliminary share of a finite future and of a finite destiny, but holds
back to himself the ultimate future and ultimate destiny of the
events which comprise the past and present.

God, Time and Eternity

The notion of the futurity of God and his Kingdom most emphatically does not "remove" God to the future. It does not
mean that God is only in the future and was not in the past or
is not in the present. Quite to the contrary, as the power of the
future he dominates the remotest past. Neither does God's futurity exclude every idea of eternity. Certainly it is opposed to
the Greek idea of eternity which was an everlasting present
without change. In this sense, Plato and Parmenides conceived
of a timeless eternity. Eternity is not timelessness. The God of
the coming Kingdom must be called eternal because he is not
only the future of our present but has been also the future of
every past age. God assigned to each present its own historical
future; this future in turn has become past for us. Because he is
the power of the ultimate future, God has released to each single event its actual historical future. In relation to past and
present, God is constantly bringing himself back into his own
eschatological futurity.

The very essence of God implies time. Only in the future of
his Kingdom come will the statement "God exists" prove to
be definitely true. But then it will be clear that the statement
was always true. In this impending power the coming God was
already the future of the remotest past. He was the future also
of that "nothing" which preceded Creation.

The process philosophy of Whitehead and Hartshorne made
the contribution of incorporating time into the idea of God.
Theirs was an enormous achievement. But we cannot agree
when Whitehead suggests that the futurity of God's Kingdom
implies a development in God. It is true that, from the viewpoint of our finite present, the future is not yet decided.
Therefore, the movement of time contributes to deciding what
the definite truth is going to be, also with regard to the essence

of God. But — and here is the difference from Whitehead —
what turns out to be true in the future will then be evident as
having been true all along. This applies to God as well as to
every finite reality. God was present in every past moment as
the one who he is in his futurity. He was in the past the same
one whom he will manifest himself to be in the future. What
distinguishes the present argument from Whitehead's philosophy is the ontological priority of the future as this priority is
evident in the idea of God as the one who is coming.

These thoughts provoke another question about the futurity
of God. Is God future in himself or does he merely appear to
be future in relation to our, and perhaps every other, finite
standpoint? Obviously, the very idea of future is relative to
present and past. So it might be argued that the power of the
future is simply the way in which God relates himself to time-
bound man. But this is not adequate. We must go farther and
say that God is in himself the power of the future. The reason
for this is that the very idea of God demands that there be no
future beyond himself. He is the ultimate future. This in turn
suggests that God should be conceived as pure freedom. For
what is freedom but to have future in oneself and out of oneself? In his freedom, God is present to himself and keeps present to himself everything that is past, of which he has been the
future. Now, when we say that he *was* the future of his past
creatures, we are speaking according to our finite experience
of time. Because there is no future beyond God, his having
been the future of his past creatures has not, for him, passed
away. He remains the future of the whole of the past and keeps
present to himself his having been the finite future of every
finite present which has now become past. Thus he keeps his
past creatures in the present of his future.

Now we can return to the Greek concept of eternity and note
that only for the one who exists as the final future is the totally
comprehensive present a meaningful idea. This present which
comprises everything is what the Greek philosophers meant by
eternity. Thus the idea of eternity is not neglected in our considerations. It is moved into a larger understanding of reality
that does not omit the temporal dynamics from the idea of
eternity. Eternity is not the antithesis of change. Finally, the

differences of present, past, and future are overcome in the *eschaton*. For the power of the ultimate future will not be surpassed by any other future; in its unity this power has been and still is the future of every past event. Any past event, considered strictly by itself, is not surpassed by a future other than this future. The *eschaton* is eternity in the fullest sense, and this is the mode of God's being in the coming of his Kingdom.

I have promised to say something about creation. Here again we consider the power of God's future, asking the question in a different way. How can the physical finite entities be understood as having been created by the God whose power is the eschatological future? What sense does it make when we say that all events have eventuated from the power of the future? And how does this power actually dominate not just the whole human experience of time but also the specifics of every present? We are accustomed to thinking in terms of the power of the past. The past, we are taught to believe, brings forth the future according to the reliable laws which control events. Is this conventional way of thinking at all compatible with what we have said about the power of the future?

Creation and Love

In responding to these questions in the hope of at least a tentative answer, we first look for the direction in Jesus' message. He suggests that the creative power of the future is conceivable only if we understand its actuality in terms of love. So far we have dealt in abstractions when speaking of Jesus' message of the coming Kingdom. It was possible for Jesus to interpret life comprehensively and exclusively in terms of eschatology only because Jesus discovered God's love in the imminence of the Kingdom. And how did Jesus see the revelation of God's love in the imminence of the Kingdom? God's love was revealed in the ways the presence of the Kingdom manifests itself before it comes in power. Jesus saw the revelation of God's love in his own activity of announcing the imminent Kingdom, in the manifestations of God's sovereignty in this announcement, and in the faith which the announcement of the Kingdom provoked. But in what sense is all this a revelation of God's love? The present announcement of the imminent

Kingdom of God offers man a chance to participate in God's future rather than being overwhelmed by its sudden arrival and being conquered as an adversary of that future. This is the offer of salvation which reveals God's loving concern for man. Even more than that, wherever the message of the imminent Kingdom of God is accepted, God has already come into power and man now has communion with God. The salvation which is communion with God requires nothing else than to accept the message of the imminent Kingdom of God now. Jesus was therefore able to forgive sins with no conditions attached. In this unconditional forgiveness, the power of the coming Kingdom revealed itself as creative love. Creative love, through forgiveness, opens the way to new life. The creativity of genuine love is the power of a future overcoming present and past. Again, we see love as synthesis, and reconciliation as a constitutive aspect of creation.

The creative character of love is linked to the power of the future. The idea of power alone is related to the present and moves the present into new possibilities. But these may be possibilities of evil. The idea of power by itself is ambiguous, making possible both destruction and life. But creative love is unambiguous in asserting that the present is set free to life. Love is the only real answer we have to the startling question, Why should there be anything at all rather than nothing? *Love* grants existence and grants it contingently. This means that love grants *new* existence, in spite of the self-asserting arrogance of that which already is. In love we recognize the intrinsic dynamic at work in the eventuating of contingent events from the future and releasing them in the process of time.

Why something rather than nothing? Through the centuries the Christian doctrine of creation has declared that love is the ultimate motive of God's creative activity. Theologians have not understood the interrelation of love, contingency, and future in its full radicality. But Christian theology has unfolded in the doctrine of creation the universal relevance of God's love as revealed in Jesus. A theology of creation is necessary to understand the universal import of the revelation of God's love in Jesus. Such a theology of creation shows us the divine character of this love by acknowledging it as the source of all being.

Each event presents itself to us as a work of creative love in a twofold way. First, it is a work of creative love simply in its being originated as a unique event. Second, it is a work of creative love in that it is held by creative love's ultimate intention to preserve the bond between itself and the creature. The creature-event has freedom in relation to the power of the creative love that does not let it go. The event which is the creature of creative love relates itself in some way to the existing world, but not only to the existing world. It is related also to its source in creative love. Thus the creative power proves itself to be also unifying power. The events in their relation to one another participate in the love that created them. Each preliminary integration among events and that from which they eventuated emerges as an anticipation of an ultimate unity.

We can agree with Whitehead in considering the ultimate elements of reality in terms of single occasions contingently following each other. I also share his thought that every new occasion has to prehend the world it encounters, although the new occasion cannot be derived from already existing objects. Were it so derived, it could not be genuinely new but only a different configuration of the old. I believe Whitehead's vision can be conceptualized in a more consistent way than Whitehead himself utilizes, if the contingency of the new events or occasions which occur to the existing world is described as a result of the futuristic power of creative love. In Whitehead's own theory the combined effect of a "creativity" which is attributed to matter and of ideal structures (eternal objects) tends to eliminate the novelty and contingency of events, in spite of Whitehead's efforts to offset such a tendency. The idea of love — understood not in a vague emotional way but as the creative release of new reality — is perfectly compatible with the contingency of the events that are supposed to have resulted from this origin. At the same time, the idea of love explains why contingent events are referred to the already existing world. Their relation to this world permits the development and continuity which are necessary in order that more complex and unified creatures may emerge. The powerful future of God acts in holding fast to the creature he once created. He holds fast by allotting to that creature a finite future through the

means of other creatures that are referred to it. Thus he grants
to the creature he once created a share in that reality which is
greater than itself.

Creation and Causality

The idea of the love of God as the origin of all reality does
not violate scientific descriptions of natural processes. Each
event will be understood primarily as something in itself, as a
work of creative love and not simply as a consequence of past
events or of invariable laws. The laws of causation have their
own overwhelming significance, but do not plumb the depths of
reality's foundation. Ideas of causality and the physical laws
presuppose that something exists and that events do happen.
Only the fact that each new event has to relate itself to the existing world makes it possible to describe phenomena in terms
of causality. One of Whitehead's most fascinating ideas is that
the new is not set forth by the already existing but enters subjectively into relation with what is. Thus the continuity of nature is no longer understood as the irresistible dynamic of the
already existing pushing forward, but as the building of bridges
to the past that save the past from getting lost. In this way the
familiar picture of a continuous process moving from the past
through the present and into the future becomes possible. The
combined action of innumerable events conforming themselves
to the world they enter produces the conformity of processes
that can be described in terms of causality and physical law.
In the overwhelming majority of cases, adaptation means mere
repetition and achieves no transformation of pre-existing conditions. Thus is provided not only the basis for law and causality,
but also for enduring existence. With the rise of permanent
forms, the creative love which intends the autonomy of its creation attains its preliminary end.

Even a sketch of the evolution of natural forms cannot be
attempted within the limitations of this essay. I shall content
myself to suggest some characteristic aspects of life and its evolution that are conspicuous in the light of the idea of a creative
eschaton.

In the organic life of plants and animals, "being" achieves
an intrinsic relation to the future and pushes forward to new

forms of participation in the creative origin of all being. The
particularities of organic life can be understood in terms of the
organism relating itself to the future which will change its
present condition. Especially can we understand the apparently
teleological phenomena of life by reference to anticipation of
the future. Perhaps there is a connection between the development of an intrinsic relation to the future and the development
of the intrinsic life that we call soul. Apparently no animal is
aware of the futurity of its own future. To face the future as
future is quite different from simply being related to future.
The awareness of the future as such seems to be reserved to
man.

Religion, Sin, History

A characteristic expression of this awareness is man's ability
to ask questions. Because man is able to distinguish the future
from the present, he is ahead of himself and of the existent
world. So he is able to dominate that world. It follows from this
openness for the future as future that man can participate in
the creative dynamic of the divine love. A further mark of his
being human is that man has religion – a reflective relation to
the creative power of the imminent Kingdom of God which is
distinguished from the objects in the world.

God's futurity was hidden in the beginnings of human religion. Man found himself in the presence rather than in the
absence of God. The absence of God is the negative side of his
futurity. In Jesus' message it is only *as future that God is present*. In mythical religions the divine reality was understood as
primordial existence by analogy to the extant world. The presence of the divine was felt in the primordial forms of being.
History is the catalyst which makes possible the movement
from mythical religion to the proclamation of the Kingdom.
History shattered mythical existence and enabled man to rise
to a consciousness of his own historicity as it is interrelated
with the futurity of God.

The perverse (in the literal sense of that word) apperception
of the divine reality in religious experience is only one more
form assumed by the perversion of man's relation to the future.
The perversion, of course, is the conventional perspective of

experience in which the future is understood as a prolongation of what is already existing, rather than being understood as the creative origin of reality. This perverse attitude occurs because the divine love creates autonomous forms of existence. These forms of existence in turn strive to prolong their existence. Present actualities are marked by an arrogance which blinds them to the preliminary character of their forms of being. This tendency toward self-assertion is not without a deep ambiguity. On the one hand, it reflects an assent to the particular existence received from God. But, on the other, it tends to close itself off from the future and the future's promise of change. In this tendency we may seek the roots of all absurdity, suffering, and evil which so grievously distort nature. But only in man does this enmity against the future become sin. When man asserts himself against the future, he misses his authentic existence, betrays his destiny to exist in full openness toward what is to be, and abdicates his participation in God's creative love.

All conservative persistence in established securities will be shattered and surpassed by historical change. The process of history is God's instrument in the education of humanity, bringing man to the awareness of his historicity and thus completing his creation.

The human significance of history may be seen in the history of religions. Religious experience has to do with the wholeness of experience in the light of divine reality. While the reality is differently understood at different times, it is always an integrating force, relating the existence of individuals and groups into a meaningful whole. The archetypes of myth arose in the history of man's experience of divine reality, and just as surely were these myths refuted by the same process of historical change. Only the experience of the God who is the power of an ever-renewed future will do. In relation to the God of the power of the future, man is free: free for a truly personal life, free to accept the provisionality of everything, free with regard to nature and society, free for that creative love that changes the world without destroying it. This creative love proceeds from freedom and is directed toward affirming and creating freedom in the world. If the unity of mankind, which is the pur-

pose of history, one day becomes a reality, it will be achieved
by this love.

Trinitarian Language

Now something more should be said about the idea of God.
What I have said about the word " God " has been informed
by Jesus' message of the imminent Kingdom of God and by an
awareness that we live in a historical epoch which most definitely does not take traditional concepts of God for granted.
In reinterpreting the idea of God, it was necessary to think of
creation in reference to the *eschaton* rather than in reference
to a primordial past. We thus understand all being and events
as eventuating from the ultimate future. As we have noted,
this conception of divine power does not violate or compete
with the physicist's quest for natural causes. Our considerations
are based on a reversal of the time sequence usually presupposed in notions of causality. In contrast to formulations about
natural order, which describe the impact of past conditions on
present and future, we have suggested an idea of creation
which understands the present — and each present now past —
as resulting from its future. This approach to an eschatological
doctrine of creation culminates in the idea of divine love. God
in his powerful future separates something new from himself
and affirms it as a separate entity, thus, at the same time, relating it forward to himself. The autonomous event does not exist
in isolation but is creatively related to the freedom of the future. The past is not the dead past. Because of this activity of
divine love, we are justified in calling the God of Jesus the living God. He has no unity or being apart from the activity of
his life in which he separates another being from himself while
still keeping it alive by maintaining its relation to himself.

The reality of God, then, is the creative arrival of this powerful future in the event of love. In his creative, redeeming, and
sustaining arrival, God's future demonstrates his power. This
can be clarified by reference to the trinitarian language about
God that is common in the Christian community. In Jesus this
life of divine love is revealed in a trinitarian form. God is not
an existing entity but is the future of his coming Kingdom. As

this future, he was and is present through that man, Jesus, who testified to the coming Kingdom of God. Through this man God is present to the world as the spirit who gives freedom and life by creating faith. This faith is man's awareness of the quiet relatedness of everything to the origin of all life. The trinitarian distinctions are based on the difference between future and present. As we have seen, future and present — and consequently the "persons" of the Trinity — are comprehended in the unity of God.

In this light, we see the contrast between the trinitarian concept of God and the idea of God as taught by philosophical monotheism in classical antiquity. The trinitarian concept describes the particular unity of the living God, while philosophical monotheism conceived of the dead or static unity of a supreme being as an existing entity indistinguishable within itself. The trinitarian idea of God is congruous with historical process, while the notion of a supreme entity speaks of a "divine thing" outside man's history. The trinitarian doctrine describes the coming God as the God of love whose future has already arrived and who integrates the past and present world, accepting it to share in his own life forever. The trinitarian doctrine is, therefore, no mere Christian addition to the philosophical idea of God. Rather, the trinitarian doctrine is the ultimate expression for the one reality of the coming God whose Kingdom Jesus proclaimed.

CHAPTER II

The Kingdom of God and the Church

American fascination with language about "the secular city" focuses Christian attention most emphatically upon the world. If we examine the language more carefully, however, we discover that the "secular city debate" is a dispute about the nature of the Church. This should not surprise us. The truth is that the Church can only be understood in relationship to the world. The problem is that too often Christians have taken the Church seriously at the expense of denigrating the world. We can see in history the many instances in which the Church assumed a spirit of superiority, as though the Christian community could get along quite well without the world. Now we must understand that the connection between Church and world is by no means accidental; the Church's relationship to the world is determinative for her authentic vocation.

From a purely descriptive viewpoint, it is obvious that its relationship to the society which is *not* ecclesiastical is decisive for the self-understanding of the Christian community and of individual Christians. The very concept of a Christian community presupposes some other larger community. Sociologists of religion have noted the various ways in which the Church conceives of its relationship to society: the Church opposed to the world of the secular community; the Church as part of that world; the Church as the transforming agent of that world. These different ways in which the Church has understood its relationship to society are of more than sociological interest.

The relations of the Church with the world, with secular society, are essential for every understanding of the Church. The interrelationship of Church and world is foundational for the doctrine of the Church to be outlined in the present argument.

The central concern of the Church, and the primary point of reference for understanding the Church, must be the Kingdom of God. That is, the Kingdom must be the central concern of the Church if the Church is to remain faithful to the message of Jesus. And this Kingdom of God, according to Jesus' proclamation, points toward the future of the world, of all humanity. The message of Jesus is definitely not limited to the future of a community of believers. What warrant is there for speaking of the Church as the new people of God or the New Israel? Such language is justified only if the Church is related essentially to the Kingdom of God. And since the Kingdom of God is to be expected as the future of the whole world, such language is justified only in terms of the Church's relation to the world.

What we have said so far should meet with little disagreement. Even those people who believe the Church is essentially opposed to the world can agree. For opposition is itself a kind of relationship and, in their view, this relationship is decisive for understanding the Church. There is an element of truth in saying the Church is opposed to the world. But it is far from the whole truth and, taken in isolation, it becomes false. The idea of opposition cannot be primary in our understanding of the relationship between Church and world. The formal reason for this is that the notion of opposition tends to contradict itself by regarding the opposition (a form of relationship) as essential for a true understanding of the Church. Even more important, the idea of opposition neglects the universalist thrust in the notion of the Kingdom of God.

The expectation of the Kingdom of God explains the factual inseparability of Church and world. This suggests that the idea of God's coming Kingdom might be the appropriate starting point for a theological understanding of the Church. The argument proceeds in this way: Since every conception of the Church that disregards its relatedness to the world remains one-sided, and since only the vocation of the Church for the Kingdom of God explains theologically the essential character of her relatedness to the world; therefore, the whole of the ecclesiological thematic can be brought into perspective only from the viewpoint of the Kingdom of God.

The Future of the World

This is clarified if we consider the early Christian understanding of the Church as an eschatological community, a community of high expectation and hope. The Church was regarded as an anticipation of the new mankind, a mankind under the rule of God and his Spirit. This renewing Spirit of God was expected to be poured out in the last days upon everyone, but it was also believed that the Spirit was now present in the Church. Therefore, in both anticipatory and present senses, the Church thought of itself as the new people of God and the New Israel. Only if we take these eschatological titles seriously can we understand the nature and vocation of the Church in relation to the Kingdom of God, which is the future of the entire world. In this light, the existence of the Church is of utmost significance for all mankind, not simply for those who are members of the institution. The "Constitution on the Church" of Vatican II is correct in saying the Church is destined to reflect the light of the nations, who is Christ.

We hasten to say what this does not mean. It does not mean that the Kingdom-oriented vocation of the Church gives it some special ecclesiastical light and authority. Light and authority are not possessions of the Christian community to have and to hold and to reinforce feelings of superiority over the world. No, the Church is true to its vocation only as it anticipates and represents the destiny of all mankind, the goal of history. Whatever significance the Church has for the world depends upon the degree of the Church's devotion to this universal and humanizing vocation. Any narrowing of the universal vocation of the Church, any deviation from its character as an eschatological community, results in depriving the Church of its social significance. Then the Church becomes an institution concerned only with the religious needs of some people, needs which are obviously vanishing today among the majority of men. Because the Church has in so many ways narrowed her vocation and deviated from her hope, many responsible people wonder out loud if the Church has not become obsolete. Theology is challenged by the sad appearance of the empirical Church as a hangover from another historical period. The appropriate response to this challenge is to be found in a new emphasis upon the Church as an eschatological community pioneering the future of all mankind. (Of course, to theologize about the Church in this way is not the same thing as reshaping the empirical Church along these lines. But we will have something to say about the re-formation of some practical aspects of the Church's life later on.)

Christ and Destiny

If in our ecclesiology we understand the Church in relation to the imminent Kingdom of God — as this was understood in early Christianity — our doctrine of the Church cannot begin from the viewpoint that the Christian community is simply a group of individuals united by a common faith. The Church is not primarily an association of individuals of common religious interests and convictions. Protestantism has been very weak in this connection. The idea of *congregatio sanctorum* or *fidelium* has usually tended toward the distorted notion that the Christian community is primarily concerned with itself and with the piety and salvation of its members. Against the more superficial congregational ideas of the Church, it has been emphasized rightly that the community of Christians is based upon the communion each one has with Jesus Christ. Because of the one Christ in whom all Christians participate, there should be community among Christians and only one community comprising all Christians. These are important and correct points. However, they are still far too narrow as a basic description of the essence and destiny of the Church.

The emphasis upon communion with Christ is ambiguous, especially if Christ is conceived as the redeemer and savior of the individual or of a group of believers. This still suggests the idea of the Church as a particularly religious community isolated from, or only accidentally related to, the world and the larger society. Wherever the idea of communion with Christ has been made the ultimate basis for a doctrine of the Church, we can see — at least in theological interpretation — that splendid isolation of religion from society. This does not mean we throw out the idea of communion with Christ, as though it had nothing to do with our understanding of the Church. If we properly understand the meaning of the title " Christ," communion with Christ can point toward a more profound and exciting idea of the Church. The title " Christ " and Jesus' central concern with the imminent Kingdom are inextricably related. Jesus' whole ministry was determined by his proclamation of the coming Kingdom of God, and the title " Christ " refers to the vicarious execution of God's own rule. Therefore, communion with Christ is identical with one's dedication to the Kingdom of God as the future of the world. Within the context of proclamation and expectation of God's Kingdom, the idea of communion with Christ reveals its genuine meaning and avoids privatized notions of religious communion. And so we return to the insight that our understanding of the Church must start with the Kingdom of God and the final destination of human history.

Two Confusions

Does the Church, as a particular association, have an essential contribution to make to the whole society? Certainly the Kingdom of God is not the Church. Indeed it is quite possible to conceive of the Kingdom of God without any Church at all. The Kingdom of God is that perfect society of men which is to be realized in history by God himself. In Revelation, Saint John the Divine envisions such a society in which there is no need for church or temple. At that time, everybody will know the will of God and live in perfect response to it. It is clear that the Church is not to be equated with the Kingdom of God, nor vice versa. Before we go on to consider why the Church is now necessary for the sake of God's Kingdom, we should examine more closely the tenacious tendencies in the history of Christianity to confuse the distinction between Church and Kingdom. Sometimes the Church has been identified with the King-dom; at other times it has been said that the Church is the present form of the Kingdom, as distinguished from the King-dom's future fulfillment. The second confusion is as bad as the first.

The more sober doctrines of the Church have usually rec-ognized *some* difference between the Church and God's King-dom. But the main traditional schemes of ecclesiology too readily assumed that the Church (or a particular church) is the present, albeit imperfect, form of the Kingdom of God. Frequently, theologians who made this assumption utilized an-other distinction, namely, between the Kingdom of God and the Kingdom of Christ. The Church, it is said, is the Kingdom of Christ, while the Kingdom of God remains hidden beyond the Church and is to be revealed in its glory only in the eschat-ological future. The distinction between the Kingdom of God and the Kingdom of Christ is a difficult exegetical problem posed by the New Testament, particularly Pauline, literature. But the distinction between the two can hardly constitute a substantial difference. There is no competition between the Kingdom of God and the Kingdom of Christ. Christ's rule is nothing else than the preparing of the way for the Kingdom of God. Where Christ rules, the Kingdom of God is already dawning. This is certainly the manner of speaking about the Kingdom which corresponds with the message of the historical Jesus. It is as improper to call the Church the present reality of God's Kingdom as it is to identify the Church with God's Kingdom.

Kingdom Against Church

Christ points the Church toward the Kingdom of God that is beyond the Church. To the degree that the Church follows his pointing and heeds his reminder, the Kingdom of God will manifest itself through the Church. But note that this is quite different from attributing to the Church in its established struc-tures the dignity of being the Kingdom of Christ. The rule of Christ is effected wherever man becomes aware of the coming Kingdom of God and lives in accord with that awareness. This may happen in the Church. It should be expected to happen in the Church. But the rule of Christ cannot be identified with the Church's existence as an organized community in the world. The theological identification of the Church with the Kingdom of Christ has all too often served the purposes of ecclesiastical officials who are not attuned to the Kingdom of God. Many Christians, especially church leaders, like to think they are in possession of the truth, or at least that they possess the ultimate criterion of the truth. Because they feel themselves to be so indispensably related to the very Kingdom of Christ, they fail to recognize the provisional character of all ecclesiastical organizations. They are unable to stand humbly before the coming Kingdom of God that is going to bring about the final future of the world. They are blinded to the ways in which even now, proleptically, the future manifests itself in the world (and not just in the Church, nor even always through the Church). Precisely because the Church mistakes herself for the present form of the Kingdom, God's rule has often had to manifest itself in the secular world outside, and frequently against, the Church.

2

The doctrine of the Church begins not with the Church but with the Kingdom of God. But what is this Kingdom of God to which the Church is to be devoted in faithfulness to her vocation? Is it merely a formalistic idea about God's ruling over everybody and everything? Such a formalistic idea is hardly an adequate object on which the Church's self-understanding can be honed. The truth is that the idea is not so formalistic at all. The rule of God, sovereignty, provides unity among those who are subject to its power. Note, then, that the rule of God requires unity among men. (This, of course, is closely related to the insight that God himself is One.) Furthermore, this unity among men cannot be coerced; it cannot be enforced by violence. Such a forced unity would not testify to the Creator of man and world for human nature cannot be ultimately opposed to the Creator and his rule. Yet a rule by violence or coercion means that the subjects are by nature opposed to the rule. In our own history we have seen that such suppression does not last. It carries within itself the seeds of its own destruction. Such a rule will either be overthrown eventually or it will destroy by terror the lives of its subjects. In the latter instance, the rule does not last because there is no longer anything left over which to rule.

Love Fills the Forms

The only unity among men that does not bear the seeds of its own destruction is the unity that is brought about by justice and by caring for one another. It is not accidental that the Kingdom of God, according to the Old Testament, is expected in the form of establishing law and justice in the society of man. A kingdom of true justice would bring the fulfillment of man's social destiny within the emerging unity of mankind. At the same time, such a kingdom would satisfy the needs of each individual. This ultimate justice cannot be produced by a law in its abstract generality. While we must not despise the legal forms of life, neither should we think that, by themselves, they can provide ultimate justice for the individual. Laws cannot achieve the justice we seek precisely because they are abstract and general. Only care for the individual achieves true justice; legal formulations must be subordinated to this justice. Laws serve justice, but they do not constitute justice. So Jesus explained the will of God by the commandment of love. Love effects that unity among men which expresses itself in legal forms but which is always more than those forms. Love fills the legal forms with life and thus achieves true justice.

The Kingdom of God, far from being merely a formalistic idea, is the utterly concrete reality of justice and love. But let no one think that the Kingdom of God is therefore primarily concerned with the subjective behavior of individuals, rather than with the institutions of social life. A subjectively individualistic idea of justice and love becomes especially dangerous if it is combined with a basic dualism between religion and society. Subjective behavior and social institution must never be separated. Subjective behavior is related always to social institutions and, in most instances, is the enactment of the social forms of life. One of the problems in much academic writing about ethics is that subjective behavior and its motivation are evaluated in an abstract way in terms of the individual not interfering with the established forms of social life. But the Kingdom of God speaks in a radical way also to those established social forms. Justice and love are relevant not only to the individual but, primarily, to the structures of human interaction. Obviously, then, the Kingdom of God is pointedly political.

The Political Vision

Perhaps we ought to work for the political form in which the Kingdom of God can be realized. Certainly we would have precedents in the various historical attempts to build a theocratic form of society. These theocratic societies, however, usually operated with oppression and terror. Thus they demonstrated that they were not the Kingdom of God. The Kingdom is not yet the way it is among men; it is not the present reality. Our present world with its injustices, brutalities, and wars demonstrates the gap between itself and the Kingdom of God. The utter realism of the Biblical literature is evident in its proclamation of the Kingdom of God as the *coming* reality. No matter how well things were going, no matter how intimately the communion with God was felt, the Kingdom of God was announced as the future, the coming, Kingdom. In the light of the futurity of God's Kingdom, it is obvious that no present form of life and society is ultimate.

This insight does not paralyze political activity. The future Kingdom of God — because it is God (for God's Being cannot be separated from his rule) — demands obedience already in the present. The future of the Kingdom releases a dynamic in the present that again and again kindles the vision of man and gives meaning to his fervent quest for the political forms of justice and love. The new forms that are achieved will, in contrast with the ultimacy of God's Kingdom, turn out to be provisional and preliminary. They will in turn be called upon to give way to succeeding new forms. Superficial minds might think that the political quest is therefore futile. They fail to recognize that the satisfaction is not in the perfection of that with which we begin but in the glory of that toward which we tend. We possess no perfect program, but are possessed by an inspiration that will not be realized perfectly by us. It is realized provisionally in the ever-renewed emergence of our striving in devotion to history's destiny.

But how do we know what is better as we move toward the best? The measure by which we evaluate the transformations of political and social forms of life is the measure of love. In Jesus' teaching, love is the final norm of justice. Love is equipped to be the measure of justice because it is not an abstract principle. Love is a dynamic reality producing, in an ongoing process, new forms of human unity; each form surpasses its predecessor and anticipates its successor. Jesus insisted upon the present and radical relevance of God's coming Kingdom. He identified love as its ultimate norm, and, by exemplifying the love of God in his own life and death, Jesus proved to be the expected *christos,* the Messiah of God, who shall establish God's Kingdom on earth. The dignity of Jesus as the Christ, as the Messiah, is a result of the way he represented and still represents for all of humanity the Kingdom of God as already determining and transforming the present by creative love. All the words and formulas of Christology have truth to the degree they express how the future of God's Kingdom became determinative for the present of Jesus' life and, through him, for the history of mankind. In Jesus' radical devotion to the Kingdom of God, that Kingdom became present in him. In him the Kingdom is present to all men.

The Marxist Critique

Now we are ready to talk about the function of the Church. First it was necessary to recall the social relevance of the Kingdom of God, the centrality of the Kingdom in Jesus' message, and the key role of the Kingdom in all Christological statements about his life. The function of the Church, put quite simply, is a preliminary function. By this we mean that the existence of the Church is justified only in view of the fact that the present political forms of society do not yet provide the ultimate human satisfaction for individual or corporate life. If the present social structures were adequate, there would be no need for the Church. For then the Kingdom of God would be present in its completeness.

The Marxist explanation for the continuing existence of religious communities is therefore correct. At least it is correct in this limited but important sense: even in socialist societies a special religious community continues to exist because, and as long as, the political structure has not yet realized the ultimate form of human life, of true humanity. The mistake of the Marxists is not in the way they characterize the social function of the churches (or of other religious communities). The Marxist mistake is rather in the illusion that the truly humanistic form of society can be achieved definitely by man, and that it can be achieved in a short historic period. Paradoxically, we must insist that it is part of the very *condition* of true humanity, in the present provisional state of reality, to understand that no form of human life is exclusively and ultimately the realization of humanity. A clear witness to this understanding of our historic limitation is the existence of many actions and institutions that are clearly inhuman. The recognition that man is not God is still an essential condition of true humanity. The Kingdom of God will not be established by man. It is most emphatically the Kingdom of *God.* Any effort to make man appear to be more than he can be in his historically preliminary moment inevitably makes man less. Man is not exalted, but degraded when he falls victim to illusions about his power.

An Honest Institution

Man in his individual and corporate life needs honest institutions. An honest institution is one which uncovers the limitations of all present forms of social and political life and which brings man into relation with the ultimate reality that comprises his own ultimate destiny. This relation must be effected by confronting candidly — not by evading — the shortcomings and limitations of man's present life. The Church is to be such an honest institution. The Church brings individual members of society into relationship with the final destiny of mankind, with the Kingdom of God. This is done through communion with Jesus in whom the Kingdom of God was already present. In its mission, the Church proclaims the knowledge of Jesus' universal significance, as the revelation of God in the midst of history. By its sacramental community with Jesus, the Church makes it possible for contemporary man to share in the hope for the ultimate fulfillment of humanity. At the same time, the Church nurtures no illusions which evade the preliminary character in all present realizations of human life. In this sense, there must be the Church as a particular religious community alongside other communities and institutions. The Church is necessary so long as the social and political life of man does not provide the ultimate human fulfillment that the Kingdom of God is to bring in human history. In this way we see that the Church is not eternal, but is necessary for the time this side of the Kingdom.

The Church has a vital critical role to play in society. The Church must always witness to the limitations of any given society. The very existence of the Church depends upon its playing this critical role. When this critical witness is abandoned, the Church becomes superfluous. In that case, the Church remains only as an institution catering to the religious needs of a fast-diminishing minority that needs that sort of thing.

There is an even greater danger, however. The Church can sever itself from the problems of the society. At first sight, it may seem that such a severance from social processes is really a radical form of criticism. It might be argued, for instance, that secular society can never attain the "higher" goals which are the proper concern of the Church. But, in fact, what looks like a radical criticism of society turns out to be the most dreadful and conservative conformity to society. When the Church is isolated from the social sphere, history demonstrates that its social function really continues, whether the Church is aware of this social function or not. The social function of the Church becomes a perverted dynamic that diverts attention from the human situation into the realms of otherworldly fulfillment. Thus the churches that claim to be occupied exclusively with "spiritual" matters, that disdain any involvement in political questions, become bastions of conservatism. The energies that could be channeled into changing the actual life of the society are diverted to a supernatural sphere. There is no shortage of examples which illustrate the strange alliance of churches with the established powers of society. These strange and unholy alliances have distorted grievously the history and self-understanding of the Christian community.

We cannot argue with the Marxist critique of religion at this point. We can only confess the fault. Because of the Church's emphasis on otherworldliness, it could be and was exploited by the several social establishments in their passion for their own perpetuation. The Marxist criticism, however, fails to see that this is a distortion of the Church's relation to society. The distortion is deadly and subtle. It is so subtle that many Christians also are incapable of detecting it. For the distortion which results in separation from society is disguised as a radical criticism of society for the sake of the Kingdom of God. But the apparent sharpening of the critical difference between the Church and the world actually results in the Church's abandoning its critical role. The Church dare not confuse criticism with aloofness. It must take the present social and political forms with greatest seriousness and appraise them in the light of the coming Kingdom of God. The coming Kingdom is not some otherworldly phenomenon; it is the destiny of present society. In this way we can articulate the difference of the Church from the world within the world itself. The difference must be articulated for the sake of the Kingdom, but also for the sake of the society. In fact, these two are seen to be the same. We are not called to choose between concern for the Kingdom and concern for society. Rather, in concern for society we are concerned for its end and destiny, namely, for the Kingdom of God. To act for the sake of the Kingdom is to act for the sake of society, and, in so doing, we act to the benefit of the Church. A concern for the Church that is not first of all a concern for the Kingdom of God is inevitably inverted and leads, as we have seen, to the Church's becoming superfluous.

Demythologizing Politics

The existence of the Church as a distinct institution in contemporary society is justified to the degree that the Church carries out its critical and constructive function of pointing society toward its fulfillment in the Kingdom of God. The Church has an essential place in society because she is concerned with the ultimate destiny of man and society. The Church exercises her function in two ways. On the one hand, a distinct Church institution prevents the political organization and its representatives from claiming ultimate human significance for themselves. It forces a more realistic admission of their preliminary character. The Church has the task of demythologizing the political myths of a given time and of sobering up those who become drunk on their possession of power. She also exercises her function in a second and positive way. By witnessing to the future fulfillment of humanity in God's Kingdom, the Church helps to stir the imagination for social action and to inspire the visions of social change. In a time when many intelligent people doubt that mankind has a future, the Church must more urgently and persuasively proclaim the Kingdom of God.

In the history of Christianity, this positive contribution has frequently had to come from the so-called sectarian movements. It must be admitted that in many instances these sectarian movements were fulfilling the real function of the Church. At the same time, we should not be carried away into saying that the Church must always be revolutionary. The future of God's Kingdom, in its saving of this world, is related to this world is an assertive manner. This means that, for the sake of the Kingdom of God, the Church must resist the temptation to disdain the social and cultural heritage. A disdain for, and wasting of, this heritage is usually connected with revolutionary movements. We should not be reckless with history. Therefore, the word " revolution " should be used with caution in describing the Church's role in society. Certainly we do want to say that the Church is eager for change. She recognizes that the heritage cannot be saved by attempting to conserve it

in its given forms. The heritage can only be saved by further
development of its human significance. The Church also recognizes that change is not a mechanical process of inexorable
growth. Indeed, change can mean loss as well as progress. But
the unavoidable fact is that there can be no life, neither individual nor social, without change. That means there can be
no real life without mastering the dynamic urge of every given
situation toward a new manifestation of human life. Does the
Church as a distinct institution in society have a future? The
answer depends on her belonging to the ultimate future of man
and society, both of which wait for a more appropriate realization.

3

The Church in a secular society provides the individual with
an opportunity to participate now in the ultimate destiny of
human life. This is the Church's mandate and, if she is faithful
to it, her special contribution. All secular forms of social life
can offer only a preliminary satisfaction; the Church confronts
the person with the ultimate fulfillment of life promised in the
coming of God's future. Because the Church gives the individual a share in this future salvation, the life of the Church
even now should produce signs of the anticipated wholeness
and integrity of human life. Such wholeness is not limited to
the individual's well-being, but encompasses also social institutions and their administration. In connection with human
wholeness and integrity — a consequence of participating in
the coming Kingdom of God — we can speak of the presence of
the Holy Spirit. The Spirit, the origin of all life, reveals himself as promised to the Christian community.

What does it mean to say the Church is endowed with the
Holy Spirit? It is not enough simply to assert the Spirit's presence because Christians have asserted it through the centuries.
We must also resist modern tendencies to narrow the reality
of the Spirit. Sometimes the Spirit is spoken of as though he
were a somewhat obscure principle of a supernatural knowledge and piety that is unobtainable in ordinary human ways.

We reject the notion that the Holy Spirit is some kind of stop-gap for the weaknesses of human argument. The Spirit is not a cover-up for the abandonment of reason, nor is the Spirit a disguise for the irrationality of religious subjectivity. His activity is not restricted to the inwardness of religious experience.

Spirit and Resurrection

The Holy Spirit is the Almighty God himself, and his breath blows through all creation. In the Old Testament especially, he is understood as the origin of all life. This corresponds to our earlier considerations about life itself being related to the future, a future which is ultimately the future of God's Kingdom. In this light, it is meaningful to speak of the Spirit of God as he who keeps all living creatures alive. Likewise, particularly intense manifestations of the mystery of life are to be attributed to special endowments of the Spirit. Once we understand the intimate connection between the whole range of the phenomena of life and the divine Spirit, we can understand the close kinship between New Testament statements about the Spirit and the proclamation of Jesus' resurrection. This kinship is notably accented in Paul who argues that, since a new life has appeared in Jesus' resurrection, the resurrection event pours forth the divine Spirit. The very proclamation of this event is full of spiritual power, and faith in this proclamation receives the Spirit of life. The life received is the life that has overcome death.

When Paul speaks of " spiritual " life, he has explicit reference to the Holy Spirit. The spiritual life, or spiritual body, remains in unity with the Spirit, the source of all life, and thus it will never die again. This is not true of the first and ordinary life. The first life yearns for eternity, it is true, but it is also doomed to death, because it has separated itself from the origin of all life, from the divine Spirit. And yet eternity is the mystery in all life, present in it for the time it lasts. The present mystery of eternity can only be brought to fulfillment by the eternal Spirit. In this bringing to fulfillment, the Spirit perfects our present existence by giving to it its wholeness and integrity. This same Spirit is indeed present and creative in all life.

But he has entered into a lasting unity with the resurrected
Lord and, therefore, is poured into the hearts of those who
have communion with Jesus the Lord by faith.

By faith in Jesus, Christians participate in the fullness of the
life that has been granted to him. This is true in spite of the
antagonisms of their present situations which, it may be said,
give them a share in Jesus' cross. Unity with Jesus is accom-
plished in personal trust. This trust accepts Jesus' own invitation
to faith and is expressed in accepting this invitation to his Eucharistic meal. For the Christian, this unity with Jesus is the
pledge of his own future participation in the renewed life. By
faith and hope, by sharing in the Eucharistic banquet which
both recalls the promise and anticipates its fulfillment, the
Christian participates in the resurrected life of Christ even
now.

Flashes of Eternal Joy

The presence of God's future through faith and hope embraces the entire world. It is not limited to the few believers.
The Spirit of the new life, who fulfills the meaning of all life,
culminates in love. We must acknowledge frankly that, in the
course of Christian history, the behavior of Christians has frequently, if not usually, suppressed the Spirit of love. The instru-
ments of suppression have sometimes been dogmatic zeal, self-
righteousness, or deadly acedia. Christians have a full share of
the weaknesses and temptations of human nature, all of which
have been marshaled against the work of the Spirit. Even the
Christian faith itself has been perverted into just another way
of haughtily separating oneself from the unhappy rest of mankind. When, in these and other ways, the Spirit of love is ab-
sent, faith and hope are feeble and inauthentic. Yet we know
that there is no life that does not live from God's love. God's
love alone is the reason why anything is, the reason why the
future relates itself to the present. To the degree that the nar-
rowness and seclusion of our lives is overcome by the power
of God's Spirit, love penetrates our life. This penetration need
not come as a great wave of emotional affection. But the penetration of love will be distinguished by generous concern for

other people. Where men cherish human life and serve the needs of the brother and call one another to their human dignity, there is the Spirit of love overcoming our fatal isolation. Faith and hope open our lives to the venture of love. Creative love, unloosed by faith and hope, has the power to pierce this fragile and mortal life with flashes of eternal meaning and joy. Thus we can know now the peace of wholeness and integrity.

The power of love is neither the possession nor the prerogative of the churches. In fact the churches often succumb to a stuffy atmosphere that does not permit the free breath of life and love. Yet it is the glorious vocation of the Church to witness to the freedom of the Spirit. The Church bears the memory and the message of the Spirit who quickens all creation and who intends to overcome the misery, absurdity, selfishness, and acedia of life. The failure and suffering that alienates so many human beings from their destiny of eternal joy shall be conquered by the power of the Spirit. Wherever the freedom of the Spirit breaks through — outside the churches or within — life is given new integrity. In spite of all Christian shortcomings, the Church of Christ still carries the promise that the Spirit of life will not manifest himself just occasionally, but will be given permanently.

Spirit and Healing

The larger, " main line " churches are sometimes ashamed of the implications of the truth they declare. It is clear, for instance, that the Spirit is to have a healing, integrating impact on life in all its dimensions. Yet this insight has often become a specialty of small sectarian movements, because the larger churches were embarrassed by it. The giver of life is One and life is essentially wholeness. Thus the presence of the Spirit is opposed to the disintegrating tendencies in our existence. We must see the connection between mental peace, and even physical health, and the presence of the Spirit. He is the source and perfection of all life. There is no magic involved. We can understand that mental peace granted by the Spirit can change also the physical conditions of life in this mortal body. This whole subject of healing is made treacherous if we fall prey to delusive exaggerations that ignore the mortality of present life. Our reverence for the divine majesty of the Spirit forbids also any attempt whatsoever to use prayer or other manipulations as though the Spirit could be controlled by man. After saying all this, however, we cannot deny that the presence of the divine Spirit exercises a healing influence on all dimensions of life, working toward personal integration. It might be more convenient to deny this and thus forget how much the presence of the Spirit is suppressed in the life of the churches. Christians should in their lives signal the fullness of truly human life. When that happens, it is much more suggestive and inspiring than dozens of sermons delivered by inhibited preachers.

Irreplaceable Social Contribution

It is hardly adequate to speak only of integration in private, individual lives. The integrative powers emanating from genuine Christian faith have an impact also in the public and social spheres. Faith vivified by the presence of the divine Spirit is concerned for life in common. Secular culture is marked by a progressive specialization of human activities. In this culture, it is a major social contribution to give individuals access to the wholeness of life in the presence of the eternal. This is the major contribution of the Church in society. All other contributions are secondary. What other institution is singularly concerned that individuals encounter a power granting wholeness and integrity to their lives in the face of the eternal God? God alone is the source making possible a truly human integration of life in all dimensions of social activity. This insight informs the Christian's struggle for peace and for human dignity in education, jobs, and housing. A living Church will devote herself to all these problems precisely because she is concerned for the presence of the eternal. The Church's devotion is to the impact of the future of God's Kingdom on present life in all its dimensions. The specifically social activities of the Church (its welfare organizations, child care centers, nursing and hospital establishments, schools, etc.) are subsidiary and temporary. The Church engages in these activities as a substitute for the political community. The Church's effort should be directed

toward making the state ready and able to assume these responsibilities which are appropriate to the political structures
of society. It is a strange twisting of its sense of mission when
the Church becomes jealous of the state and wants to monop-
olize certain welfare activities. The Church's satisfaction is in
stimulating the political community to accept its responsibilities. The only irreplaceable social contribution of the Church is
the personal integration of human life by confronting man with
the ultimate mystery of life, with the eternal God and his purposes in history.

A whole man is the man aware of the ultimate mystery of
life beyond our life. In this awareness, he can be whole in himself and remain superior to and untrapped by the multitude of
diversions and obligations in his present existence. He recognizes that this multitude has but a limited claim on his time
and his powers. In the presence of the eternal, the whole man
is given a sense of priorities. In Biblical piety the Sabbath is
understood in this connection. The humanizing function of the
Sabbath is seen in terms of man's need to put a distance between himself and his specialized work. He must think beyond the particularities of his occupations and understand the
place of his activities within God's comprehensive concern for
man and for the whole of human society. For Christians, the
Sabbath has been replaced by the Sunday, the day of dawning eschatological fulfillment in Jesus' resurrection. It is no
longer simply a day of repose. It is a day of heightened concern for the ultimate fulfillment of the life that began in Jesus
the Christ and is destined by its power to transform the whole
of the world. The Christian Sunday should release rays that
penetrate all the days of the week and give human dignity to
their secular occupations.

Liturgy Done by Some, for All

The eschatological splendor of the Christian Sunday should
be evident in the liturgical life of the community. Unfortunately, this is not always the case in our churches today. In
their worship, the early Christians anticipated the eschatological praise of God by the chorus of all his creatures singing to-

gether in a renewed world. The praise of God belongs to the joy of a perfection that is granted by him. It is true that the Christian community has not yet attained that final perfection. But the community is assured a part in the glory that has appeared already in Christ. And thus the community has a part in the fulfillment of human destiny in the presence of the Kingdom of God. Even now the community delights in the presence of the Holy Spirit who will bring about the new creation. Even now the community can gather to *celebrate*. The Christian community praises God on behalf of all mankind for the eschatological perfection that he has assigned to his creation, and to man in particular, through Jesus the Christ. As we praise God for the dawning of his eschatological salvation in Jesus, so also we yearn and pray for the completion of that salvation. The liturgy of the Christian community is a vicarious activity. It is done by some but for all. It is filled with universal and eschatological significance for everyman.

The liturgy of the Sabbath or Sunday is distinct from, even separate from, the secular occupations of the week. It must be so until the eschatological salvation occurs and all preliminary forms of life are transcended. This truth can easily be distorted into a pretext for excluding secular life from the transforming influences of faith, hope, and love. The distortion is dreadfully common in the history of the Church. Nevertheless, no matter how the social reality may be changed, it still will be preliminary. The need for a distinct Sunday and a distinct Church will continue. This distinct or separate existence is not because the Church is superior to secular society or because the Church should remain untainted. Quite to the contrary, there must be a distinct Church for the sake of secular society! The Church exists for society and for all mankind. The Church forfeits her right to existence when she regards her existence as an end in itself. Secular society needs the Church. Secular society cannot remain secular — aware of its own preliminary character — without the Church as a separate institution to remind the present order of its provisionality. The Church issues this reminder in a positive way by witnessing to the wholeness of life in the presence of God. When the Church is faithful to her task she makes it possible to live in the secular world. Otherwise, secular society absolutizes its institutions, abandons its secularity, and exercises a tyranny over mankind.

4

The churches must change their structures if they are to accomplish their particular task in modern society. There is one change in particular that is utterly imperative. In this respect, a radical change is long overdue; indeed it has been urgent since the eighteenth century. The change I have in mind has to do with the authoritarian character of the older forms of Christian tradition. Authoritarian elements have permeated the life of the churches in many ways. Consider the tradition of hierarchical order or the notion of obedience, quite apart from the criticism of reason, to dogmatic formulas. Consider the view of Scriptures as divine word that must be obeyed, or the idea of worship as it has been concentrated in the proclamation of the authoritative divine word by the minister. The notion of faith as obedience is authoritarian, yet it has shaped so much of the life of the churches. Even the organizational church life has been affected, as is evident in authoritarian influences that shape the social and religious position of the minister or priest who is supposed to possess special powers. These and many other authoritarian elements prevent the Church from performing adequately in a secular society. Until they are overcome, the Church will hardly be able to make the contributions that are desperately needed in our world. Authoritarian structures in the churches have produced clericalism, dogmatism, persecutions, and divisions. The Church has lost her unity, she has failed to be the sign of truth, she has obscured the image of the one God.

No Privileged Areas

The criticism launched by the Englightenment against the authoritarian structure of Christianity was not necessarily opposed to the heart of Christian faith. We can understand, certainly, that critics as well as defenders of the Church often mistook its authoritarian form for its substance. But participation in the Kingdom of God by faith liberates man from every other ultimate authority. Man is free to judge everything. This applies not only to the political forms of life, but also to ecclesiastical organizations and formulas. The gift and privilege of freedom must be exercised with regard to the proclamations brought forth by the churches, to their doctrinal decisions, to the Biblical writings, and even to Jesus' own message. In the last instance we note that the message of God's coming Kingdom is no exception to the rule that man is exempt from all unconditional human authority. Since the message that established this freedom is itself proclaimed by man, it is open to critical examination as are all other claims to authority. In the whole of man's political and intellectual existence, there are no privileged areas exempt from critical reflection. The message of God's coming Kingdom does not need to be protected. It will pass examination. God as man's Creator is not altogether unfamiliar to man. If man turns his back to God, he can be shown to have betrayed his own nature and destiny.

As vigorously as we call for a change from the authoritarian elements in the Christian tradition, we can nevertheless understand their origins and their strong hold upon the churches. The authoritarian structure of the Church before the Reformation and even afterwards until the eighteenth century was due to the special conditions of transmitting historical facts in the ancient and medieval world. Scientific knowledge was then thought to be restricted to the realm of general and timeless propositions. The particularities of history were regarded as foreign to scientific investigation. If eyewitnesses who could be questioned were no longer at hand, one was left with the decision to believe or disbelieve a tradition that was finally based upon eyewitness evidence. In such a situation, everything depended upon the credibility of a particular tradition or of its present representatives. Any possibility of distortion of the *tradendum* in its course of being handed down to the present had to be excluded. Therefore Augustine said he wouldn't believe the gospel if he didn't first believe the catholic Church. A chief dynamic in the concern for apostolic succession of bishops was the desire to guarantee the reliability of the Christian tradition. In the ancient world, the identity and purity of the Christian tradition was secured only by authoritarian structures which regulated its process of transmission.

The More Mature Man

This situation has changed radically in modern times. The development of historical criticism and its application to the Biblical texts has in principle replaced the authoritarian structure. Ancient institutions such as episcopal succession, hierarchy, and dogma are no longer necessary; at least they are not necessary to securing conformity between contemporary proclamation and the origin of all Christian tradition, i.e., Jesus himself. Before the development of the historical examination of traditional texts, authoritarian forms were inevitable. It was natural that people desired a structure which could tie together the diverse processes in the handing down of the tradition. Then too, authoritarian structures were not so objectionable in a period that was accustomed to authoritarian institutions in every area of political and social life. With the development of methods of historical examination, such structures have become obsolete and repugnant. Authoritarian claims for certain traditions, quite apart from their historical examination or even contradicting the results of such examination, are simply no longer credible. It is important today to secure the identity and purity of the Christian tradition. But authoritarian structures are no longer necessary to the task. This end is better achieved by the continuous reexamination of the Christian origins and by confronting contemporary Christianity with the problems and results of such investigations. These problems and results should, as much as possible, be made accessible to the educated judgment of every Christian.

The freedom of the children of God is enhanced by their liberation from superfluous authoritarian structures of the Christian tradition. In this sense the Church is more mature and man has more nearly come of age. It is a remarkable fact that the liquidation of authoritarian institutions in political and social life took place in about the same period as the application of the mature historical method. Although there was presumably no direct dependence between the two developments, political and social liberties would hardly have survived within Christianity if the authoritarian character of the religious tradition had remained unchallenged. I venture the judgment that the freedom of the children of God became mature and exterted a broader influence on the transformation of social and political life only after the authoritarian form of the Christian tradition had become superfluous. If this is the case, it is even more important that the present continuation of the Christian tradition move forward within the context of free reasoning and discussion. The content and relevance of Jesus' message as well as their presuppositions in Jewish tradition must be established by unhindered critical investigation. This invites a plurality of interpretive attempts. We can expect sharp contradictions and extreme proposals for reformulating the Christian substance. But all of these attempts, while they may be disturbing to some, make a positive contribution to the ongoing endeavor to discover the meaning and relevance of the source of Christian tradition. Extremes and imbalances will be placed into perspective and receive their just measure in the process of free discussion.

Removing the vestiges of an authoritarian past will produce sometimes painful consequences in the life of the churches. But this is the price of coming of age, and the changes which accompany the pain can be welcomed heartily. We will look at the consequences in several areas of the church's life: in the proclamation and instruction, in the attitude toward doctrine, in missionary activity, in institutional order, in intra-Christian ecumenical relations, and in the approach to non-Christian religious communities.

Teaching Autonomous Persons

Dogmatic perspectives of particular denominations have no future in the renewed Church's proclamation and instruction.

The call to commitment must be based on rational information and discussion about the riches and problems in the
Christian tradition. The alternative to barren denomination-
alism is a preaching and teaching that is historically objective;
that is to say, catholic. There is in contemporary society a
widespread interest in objective information about Christianity,
its origin and its history. The professional theologian should
meet this interest by being the teacher of his community. He
should enable Christians as much as possible, and according
to their particular situation in life, to form their own personal and mature judgments with regard to the crucial points
of the Christian faith. Judgments are made, of course, without the help of the theologian. But the professional theologian's
job is to help the community make judgments in as reasonable
and mature a way as possible. In accepting this responsibility,
the professional theologian who is a parish pastor will find
himself in a better position to make use of his academic
studies. As it is today, the intellectual skills of our pastor-
theologians are often wasted in activities that are alien to
their education. The more the members of a community are
informed about the substantial points of the Christian faith
and the chief questions of their contemporary discussion, the
more they are able to participate in what happens in the
sermon.

When people are equipped to listen judiciously, the sermon
is no longer an authoritative word of God but an attempt to
reformulate the substantial truth of the Christian faith. This
reformulation is carried out in the context of contemporary
experience and understanding of reality in all dimensions of
human existence. It should be related particularly to the life
of the community which is invited to participate in the reformulation. Thus the sermon offers an example and some
guidance for the members of the community in their own
thinking about the Christian faith and its present truth. The
people should not judge blindly, and certainly they should
not uncritically parrot the ideas of their preacher. Rather they
are called to reflect in an educated and responsible way, taking into account not only theoretical information but also a

comprehensive understanding of their own life's experience. Preachers should make a special effort to speak to the concreteness of life experience. Similarly, the members of a congregation should be equipped to appreciate the liturgical expressions in which they participate. They should not be intimidated with edicts about what is proper or permitted, but should be invited to reflect on what is done in the liturgy and how it might be done better. In liturgy, as in preaching, the task is to reformulate in a way that is sensitive to the tradition and appropriate to the community's understanding of itself and its hope. Also in pastoral counseling, people should be treated as adult and autonomous persons. The goal is to offer some guidance as to how a human life can be whole in the presence of God, and to inspire the courage of action based upon the person's own mature reflection.

Missions

Christian missions are equally affected by removing the vestiges of an authoritarian tradition. Today there is a widespread and often vehement rejection of the missionary idea. Much of that rejection can be attributed to the authoritarian way many Christian missionaries acted in the past, urging conversions instead of convincing by example and argument. In most cases the task of mission today is connected closely with the ecumenical task. Christian communities in particular areas must be strengthened and helped to develop so that they may become progressive examples of, and forces for, human dignity in their societies.

Episcopacy

The backbone of the authoritarian structure of Christianity in the past was the hierarchical order. I am passing by the conflict between clergy and laity, a conflict perhaps less severe today in all the churches. I can envision the time, not far distant, when the theological specialist in the community is no longer regarded as something " other " from other members of the community. His role will be that of a specialist in theology, in exploring and applying the Christian tradition.

But the problem of the hierarchy is thornier. It has been made more so by its prominence in contemporary ecumenical discussions. As we have seen, there was a time when the hierarchical structure of the ecclesiastical organization, together with its authoritarian implications, was justified and perhaps necessary to secure the identity of the Christian tradition in the process of the tradition's transmission. But today the tradition is better preserved in other ways. The Reformation principle of the self-evident character of the Scriptures made every Christian in principle a competent reader of the Bible. It rendered a special authoritative interpretation superfluous. Thus the Reformation opened the way to a congregational understanding of the Church as a voluntary association. The congregational idea is one-sided if the self-evident character of the Scriptures is not understood to be its presupposition. Otherwise, the idea of the Church as a voluntary association disregards the dependence of every single generation of Christians upon the process of tradition. But, if we remember the idea of the self-evident character of the Scriptures and the further development of the idea by the historical-critical method, we can see that understanding the Christian community as a voluntary association is not so strange. The Church as a voluntary association of free assent clearly expresses the basic insight of Christian freedom. On the other hand, it is not simply a matter of arbitrary decision as to whether one belongs to the Christian community or not. The priority of tradition and environment, above all individual decision, has to be taken into account. If we forget this priority, we end up with an abstract picture of the Christian community, with some form of invisible Church.

. . . and Papacy

The episcopal system of church government should be taken seriously within the context of the above considerations. After the idea of episcopacy has been purged of its authoritarian elements, there remains a representative office. This important office represents not only the unity of the community as a whole, but also its connection with the Christian tradition in its development from the beginning and through all times. The same perspective applies to the papacy. It can be viewed as the highest office, representing not only the whole of present Christianity, but also its unity with the Church of the past. The papacy may have a significant and positive role in our active concern for Christian unity. Certainly we do not think of this unifying papacy in terms of an authoritarian structure, nor as a guarantee of the identity of the tradition, nor as possessing monarchical jurisdiction. It is encouraging to note that many in the Roman Catholic Church are also reconsidering the role of the papacy, with a view toward its positive contribution to Christian unity. At the most official levels, the Roman Catholic Church has made important, albeit preliminary, steps toward a transformation of her authoritarian structure. It is possible to foresee a further stage in that process that would allow us to acknowledge the significance of a unified representation of Christianity. The crucial condition of such acknowledgment is that we not surrender the treasures of Christian freedom and maturity that have been brought to light by the Reformation and by the Enlightenment.

Unity and Plurality

Finally, we turn to the authoritative character of Christian doctrines. It is a commonplace today that Christian unity does not necessarily presuppose a consensus in doctrine. But the commonplace is based on vague intuition rather than upon a thesis supported by clear argumentation. I suggest that only a nonauthoritarian understanding of the identity of the Christian tradition can support the idea that doctrinal consensus is not essential to unity. The concern for Christian identity should find its institutional form in an ongoing critical process of exploring Christian origins and their relevance for a changing world. Within this unity there is room for different and even contradictory positions that are nevertheless one in a common endeavor. Theologians of opposite opinions should try to relate to one another in a way that is an example of how the churches ought not only to coexist but to communicate in a growing sensitivity to unity. Differences in doctrine should not be viewed as points of division but as reflecting the honesty and intensity of exchange. Such differences do not prevent the process of exploring and reformulating the Christian identity. And it is this exploration and reformulation that is at the heart of the Church's function and, therefore, of the Church's unity. Because of the preliminary character of every human activity in the light of the coming Kingdom of God, the Church will continue to be engaged in this exploring and reformulating. The organization and doctrinal articulations of the Church are, like everything in which man engages, pointed toward fulfillment and therefore preliminary. The breakdown of traditional authoritarianism can be a blessing that enables the Church to see more clearly that it is a pilgrim community on the way to meeting the future of God's coming Kingdom. This awareness may bring about a new Christian unity without uniformity. Such a unity corresponds to the unity of the one God and symbolizes the eschatological solution of the most pressing problem of modern society: to achieve and preserve unity without eliminating plurality.

CHAPTER III

The Kingdom of God and the Foundation of Ethics

The teaching of Jesus, including his ethical radicalism, was dependent on his message of the imminent Kingdom of God. He viewed every aspect of life in the light of the imminent end of the world. Every preoccupation was validated or rejected in terms of its conformity to God's action. The coming Kingdom of God — this was the single, pulsating reality of Jesus' existence. All else could be lost, if only this were to be realized. And in the realization of the Kingdom all else would be saved.

The eschatological thrust of Jesus' ethics has often been treated as a distinct liability, severely limiting his teaching's relevance to the ethical problems of an apparently ongoing world. The Sermon on the Mount, for instance, is frequently dismissed as a set of rules for the age to come or, at best, a guideline for behavior in the short period immediately preceding the final victory. In either case, the ethical teaching of Jesus has little to do with our here and now. The validity of his teaching is further questioned because, after all, Jesus was proved to be mistaken about the timetable of the Kingdom's coming. The strongly eschatological character of Jesus' ethical teaching has, understandably, been an obstacle to recognizing its universal significance.

How might Jesus' teaching be understood as a revolution in ethical thought, leading to a permanent reconstruction of our ethical foundations? The answer must take the shape of an argument suggesting that the general philosophical problem of a "foundation of ethics" is related essentially, if only implicitly, to eschatology. If that case can be made, the failure of early Christian expectations for universal salvation in that time would be less disastrous. The timetable is corrected, but the viewpoint is not repudiated. Of course there will still be elements in Jesus' ethical teaching that are not applicable in a different social situation of a different historical moment. But the central eschatological thrust of Jesus' teaching would no longer loom as so large an obstacle in Christian ethics. Indeed, what appeared as an obstacle can open the way to radical and needed reconstruction.

The question, then, is whether or not there is an essential relationship between ethics and eschatology. We will first have to ask the question within the context of philosophical reflection. Tracing the philosophical quest for ethical standards, we will see whether, in its own terms, this quest suggests a connection with eschatology.

1

It is no secret that this century has produced deep uncertainty and an anxious instability in man's ethical consciousness. Since Nietzsche proclaimed the revaluation of all values, "everything that was nailed down is coming loose." People speak nervously about traditional norms and values having lost their obligatory force. Nietzsche contended that values are created by the evaluating will. History confirms his argument with an increasing arbitrariness in standards of conduct, both in individual life and in rival systems of society. At the same time we have witnessed a widespread conformity in social behavior. It may seem strange that the relativizing of ethical standards should result in conformity. But conformity here refers to that superficial adherence to conventions, bringing behavior "into line" without any deep conviction. Such conformity is to be expected when objective and unequivocal standards for human action are lost.

The proclamation of imperatives backed by divine authority is not very persuasive today. No doubt some people do not steal or commit adultery because God has forbidden such behavior. But presumably their number is fast declining. In a rationally organized world people are accustomed to act according to reasons, even if they do frequently fail to follow their better insights. To disobey an imperative that is proclaimed without clear reasons and effective sanctions will appear wrong to fewer and fewer people.

Neither can the appeal to conscience provide absolute norms for behavior, although many have attempted to make such an argument. Conscience is not exempt from change, indeed it is in many respects a highly mutable phenomenon. The most horrible atrocities against humanity have often been carried out with the best of conscience. Such is the conscience of the fanatic who has been captured by ideology. Freud maintained that conscience is but the voice of social conventions. We might want to modify that, acknowledging that conscience sometimes moves men to rebel against their own societies. But it cannot be denied that the dictates of conscience reflect the belief-system of the conscientious man, and belief-systems are constructions of the society of which he is part.

Similar criticism applies to Kant's attempt to base ethics upon the formal imperative of action according to reason. Adolf Eichmann insisted at his trial that he had always acted according to Kant's imperative. He clearly envisioned the extermination of the Jewish people as a universal law to be universally followed. Fanatics of other strains can likewise wrap themselves in Kant's formal imperative. Kant's formal ethics does not in fact provide certain guidance toward the humanistic ideal he espoused. An additional problem with the rule that one's own actions should be suitable as a principle of general legislation is that it tends to deny individuality. The individual in his particularity and in his own distinctive moment can, at least at times, behave in a way that defies formulation as a principle suited to universal application.

Needed: An Ontological Foundation

In our day there has been much discussion of the ethics of value. Although this viewpoint is not without its problems, it has presented suggestive claims for self-evident imperatives. The ethics of value offers no single or unequivocal rule but rather a variety of contending imperatives which allegedly are felt to be self-evident as "values." Philosophers such as Scheler and Hartmann have attempted to bring some order into this variety by establishing a hierarchy of values. The difficulty of this position becomes obvious when we inquire about what mode of being is to be ascribed to values. The answer given is that values have no real existence but are "attached" to the entity. For instance, the perception "delicious" is attached to a peach, "just" is attached to a person, and so forth. It is argued that, although values have no real existence of their own, they are independent of personal experience and of the objects which offer the values to our experience. But if values have no existence of their own, how can they be independent from the subjectivity of the evaluating will and from the objects which are found valuable? Since they admittedly lack being in their own right, their independence over against the evaluating subject is secure only if the values are rooted in the particularities of the valuable *object* as related to this or that *subject*. The abiding problem is to establish values independently from the arbitrariness of subjective evaluation. The dualism of being and value does not resolve the problem. We must look further for some *ontological foundation of ethical standards*. Only on such a foundation can ethical statements be distinguished from the arbitrary or authoritarian proclamation of imperatives. Only on such a foundation do ethical statements become intelligible.

An ontological foundation of ethics must be established in connection with objective analysis of human action. On the other hand, such an analysis must go beyond the mere identification of already existent patterns of behavior. That is, within the present human reality ethics must discover the *tendencies toward* the possible amelioration of present life. Honestly confronting what is, ethics must point to what is to be, what can be, what ought to be. In this connection, we can see the element of truth in the dualism of being and value. The problematic dualism itself can be superseded by ethical statements which focus on the tendencies which point beyond the given situation of the present.

The Best Starting Point

That ethics has to do with what is beyond the presently realized human condition is not a peculiar insight of our modern era. It is to be discovered in the origins of classical philosophical ethics, in the Socratic doctrine of the good. There the good was identified as that which all people lack and for which they strive. As they strive for the good, they strive for what is good *for them*. Of course people deceive themselves about what is good for them, but yet they strive for it. At least this is clear: The good is that which man does not yet possess conclusively, that which he must still strive to realize. The good thus contains in itself the difference between value and being. The good is "beyond being," Plato said. In speaking this way, Socrates and his followers were not deriving their ethics from arbitrary imperatives but from a structural description of human action. What they agreed upon in their discussion and what we can agree upon today is that the structure of human action reveals a striving for the good. No wonder those ancient ethics are so much more intelligible than the later efforts to establish an ethical foundation in imperatives. The quest for the good, seeking what is good for human beings, still provides the best starting point for ethical investigation.

Of course we cannot today simply reiterate or repristinate the Socratic and Platonic ethics of the good. That ancient ethical construct has been excoriated, notably by Immanuel Kant, for its triviality. Socratic ethics led to "eudaemonism" which, said Kant, failed to take seriously the rigid claim of the ethical principle. Eudaemonism does not recognize that ethical action is performed for the sake of the good regardless of the consequences for the acting person. As a result of Kant's withering criticism, many more recent philosophers have been prejudiced against the entire ethics of antiquity. However, at least as it touches upon Socrates and Plato, this prejudice is unfair and superficial. Eudaemonism as criticized by Kant does not characterize their position so much as it reflects a difficulty into which they were led by their concept of the good. It is the concept of the good which we must examine more closely.

If all men are seeking what is good for them but are so easily mistaken about what is good, the obvious need is for a criterion. Personal satisfaction might be such a criterion. What gives a man the deepest satisfaction and pleasure should be good for him. In this case, striving for the good and striving for happiness would be the same thing. Thus Aristotle's *Nicomachean Ethics* begins by analyzing the search for happiness and concludes that true happiness consists in virtue. And so he presented ethics as a doctrine of the virtues.

Man Alone with Himself

The problems posed by Aristotle's formulation are readily recognized. It appears that man is finally occupied only with himself instead of with the good that is different from himself, although good for him. The distinction of the good from the man for whom it is good is evident from the fact that he strives for it. If he strives for it, he obviously does not yet possess it. To seek the good is to seek something that is different from man in his present condition and that is believed to have the power of changing that condition for the better. If, on the other hand, happiness and virtue are the final objects of ethical search, man is alone with himself and with what he is going to do with himself. Precisely this distortion is a consequence of the way Aristotle posed the question of the good. That is, it was not an arbitrary or accidental distortion. The reason the ethical quest for the good was turned back upon man is that good was defined in terms of being "good for" this man or that man. Thus the criterion of the good was subjectively based in satisfaction and happiness.

Plato had recognized this problem in the *Gorgias*. There he said that pleasure does not prove the presence of the good because bad men find pleasure in the bad. Pleasure, said Plato, only *accompanies* the good, it is not the good itself. Similarly Max Scheler argues against eudaemonism that men strive "above all for values and not for the pleasure they give." Although it is true that the experience of a value is connected with a corresponding feeling of happiness, the happiness does not establish the value but follows from it. Nicolai Hartmann says that the man who pursues happiness itself will not find it, but he who "is attached to those primary values will really get it."

But these otherwise admirable statements do not get to the heart of the problem. We must still ask how are we to *determine* the nature of the good which is to be pursued. If this question were answered, it would be easier to fulfill the demand that we should seek the good for its own sake. Lacking a criterion that determines the nature of the good, ethics will continue to fall back upon the satisfaction to be derived as the best norm for action. Even heteronomous ethics do not escape from eudaemonism. Granted, they appear to escape the trap because they insist that the proclaimed norms are to be accepted on authority and are not subject to critical examination. But to the degree that the proclaimed demands lack evidence, they demand an external observance or conformity which is supposedly in the self-interest of the faithful. Conformity is conducive to reaching certain goals, whether they be forms of earthly blessedness or heavenly reward. This is the hypocrisy inherent in every heteronomous morality. Such morality is a second-rate eudaemonism because it does not even engage the critical faculties of its adherents.

The ethical quest for the good has been seen to turn man in upon himself, because the nature of the good is determined by the subjective criterion of happiness. Between happiness and the good, how can the primacy of the good be established?

Augustine and the Good

With his answer to this question Augustine moved beyond Plato and the philosophical ethics of the ancients. Augustine was an heir to the pessimistic and dualistic mood of late classical antiquity, and he ridiculed the Aristotelian and Stoic opinion attributing the predicate of the good and of true happiness to virtue. Augustine was convinced that true happiness was not to be obtained in this earthly life and therefore rejected the idea that presently attainable satisfaction should be the criterion of the good. Augustine agreed that happiness and the good are inextricably related, but he had a more modest estimate of the kind of happiness to be achieved in the present. By what criterion then might the good be identified? In answer to this question Augustine offered his doctrine of God.

The end that is to be attained for its own sake was no longer identified with happiness — as Aristotle did (*Eth. Nic.* 1097 a 34 f.) — but with God. The condition for the hope of future happiness is commitment to God. When this order is reversed and one chooses his own happiness instead of God as the goal of existence we have, according to Augustine, the precise definition of sin. Thus the structure of the ethical quest as described in Aristotle is the description of man's sinfulness. In giving God, the true good, priority over the happiness that God may grant in the future, Augustine broke the hold of eudaemonism. It is true that the concept of the good continued to imply happiness, and it is also true that Augustine occasionally spoke carelessly about man's striving after happiness. But even in these places, Augustine did not mean the perverted desire of concupiscence but the happiness that accompanies the pure desire for the good, that is, for God.

Augustine's connection of the good with the idea of God was not an arbitrary intrusion of his subjective Christian faith. In making his case, Augustine did not step outside the philosophical tradition. Plato's idea of the good had already, and not without good reason, been understood as his esoteric idea of God. If the good is to be distinguished from the happiness it grants, it must be something within itself. Thus Plato spoke

of the good as that which is beyond every existence even beyond being. The good is to be seen as the future, yet to be
fulfilled. The good then asserts an ontological priority over
against everything extant. The priority of the future over the
present, which is implied here, is of general relevance to
metaphysics. If not only all men but all things strive for the
good, as in Plato's vision, we have reason to think of the good
as the divine that rules over everything.

Otherworldly Distortion

Augustine's connecting of the good with the divine was in
continuity with the Platonic tradition, but there were significant differences also. The chief difference was Augustine's
voluntaristic idea of God, an idea derived from the Bible.
Augustine thought of God as active in contingent events and
thus in a more personal way than would fit Plato's statements
about the good. Yet, in spite of this personal element in his
idea of God, Augustine did think of God's mode of being in
terms of God's quiet enjoyment of his happiness in another
world. The otherworldly happiness of God's being is derived
from a Greek notion of the life of the gods and is in tension
with Augustine's emphasis on Biblical voluntarism in his doctrine of God. This combination of Hellenistic and Biblical views
results in the most serious inadequacy of Augustinian ethics.
Here again we encounter the dualism and the pessimism regarding the world, a pessimism which induced a tendency to
escape this world by looking for salvation in another. This was
the same tendency that so grievously marred early Christian
piety.

Augustine's eschatology was also marked by this otherworldly distortion. The original Christian eschatology, directed to a transformation of this world, had little or no influence on Augustine's concept of God. Instead he spoke of
God in his transcendence as the embodiment of the good. Of
course, this problem was by no means Augustine's personal
doing. His thought reflected a widespread attitude which had
worked such an incisive change in the original Christian idea
of God. If God is no longer understood as coming into this

world but as a being different from the world who is the goal of pious longing, then a tendency to escape the world is rooted in the very idea of God. This escapism can be overcome only if we think of God differently. He is not a transcendent and self-sufficient being, caught in his own transcendence and separated from the world. Rather he affirms the world, relating to the world not only as its creator but also as its future. All of this is most sharply articulated in the idea of God as the One who is coming to establish his Kingdom in this world.

The notion of the coming Kingdom of God complements the idea of the good. The idea of the good is essentially related to present man and his world because the good is concerned with the future of this man and his world. This relativity in the idea of the good is neglected if God is conceived of in transcendent self-enjoyment. While the transcendent character of the good is fundamental, and while the good is therefore rightly identified with God, the ideas both of the good and of God are distorted when God is thought of in such static terms. God is the ultimate good of the ethical quest, not when he is conceived in splendid self-isolation, but when he is understood as relating himself to our world in the coming of his rule. His rule, and therefore the full revelation of his existence too, is still future. This corresponds to the futurity of the good which is not conclusively possessed but always the object of our striving. Thus it may be asserted that God, as identical with the coming of his imminent Kingdom, is the concrete embodiment of the good. This good has priority over against all human striving for the good. In this sense the Kingdom of God defines the ultimate horizon for all ethical statements.

Conversion to the World

God is the ultimate good not in isolated transcendency but in the future of his Kingdom. This means that the striving for God as the ultimate good beyond the world is turned into concern for the world.

This corresponds with God's intention for the transformation of the world through his rule. Such a reversal of the pious

tendency of leaving the world behind for God's sake constitutes a *conversion to the world.* Here we see the exciting
relevance of Jesus' message about the power of God's future
upon the present. The most constructive consequence of this
conversion to the world is the Christian idea of love that affirms the present world in transforming it.

Eudaemonism is overcome decisively by this reversal, from
an escapist striving for the transcendent perfection of God to
a sharing in the dynamics of God's love for the world. Sharing in these dynamics, the Christian moves beyond the narrow concern for his own individual happiness. He realizes
that the fulfillment of his own individual life is comprehended
in the larger love that is God's affirmation of the world. He
realizes that to participate in God's love for the world is already
communion with God himself; indeed, it is the only possible
communion with God. " God is love, and he who abides in love
abides in God, and God abides in him. (I John 4:16.)

It is not true that Christian tradition has emphasized the
private enjoyment of communion with the transcendent God
to the exclusion of love for the world and for fellowmen. But,
at least at times, this has been uncomfortably close to the
truth. While preaching and theology have generally declared
that true love for God leads to love for fellowmen, they have
also given the impression that somehow these two loves are
just that, namely, *two* loves. The mere fact that they have
been distinguished in a way that makes it possible for people
to separate love for God from love for fellowmen points to
the real problem. Seldom has it been lucidly proclaimed that
love for God, no matter how piously fervent, cannot reach him
in another world. Seldom has it been proclaimed beyond equiv-
ocation that to love God can only mean to participate in the
dynamics of his love for this world and for this mankind.

The key to understanding the inextricable connection between love for God and love for fellowmen is the identity of
God's *being* with the coming of his Kingdom. Christian ethical
failure is closely related to a misunderstanding of the doctrine of God. The idea that God is an entity which has the
definite mode of its being in some transcendent realm of its

own suggested, inevitably, that love for God moves in another direction than love for fellowmen. Consider the pious literature that speaks of our "vertical" love for God and our "horizontal" love for fellowmen. Love for God, it is suggested, takes off for heaven, while love for fellowmen remains on earth. Granted that love for God is supposed to generate love for fellowmen, but they are still two distinct acts. We need more clearly to see that love for fellowmen is participation in God's love; that is to say, love for fellowmen is participation in the coming Kingdom of God. The priority of God's coming Kingdom and the possibility of our participating in the coming Kingdom is, properly understood, the meaning of grace.

Schleiermacher and the Nineteenth Century

The eighteenth and nineteenth centuries contributed another dualism in the doctrine of the ultimate good, a contribution related to the dualism of love for God and love for fellowmen. The tradition that identified God and the ultimate good was modified by Leibniz and later on by Kant, who distinguished this highest good from another highest good that was to be realized by human action. This second highest good was projected as the ideal result of man's ethical labor. In the same direction, Schleiermacher developed his ethics as a doctrine of the good. He declared the highest good to be a "complete penetration and integration of nature by and with reason." Man's dominance over nature permits him to utilize nature increasingly as a tool and as a symbol of his own destiny. Thus Schleiermacher's ethics was a philosophy of culture and of the process of its development.

The impressive fact in Schleiermacher's work is that every tendency to escape from this world is emphatically excluded. His ethics is perhaps the most prominent example of a Protestant ethics completely devoted to the world and its formation. But the motif of his thought was neither God as a transcendent good nor the Kingdom of God imminent to the world. The motif is man's acquisition of the world. Thus the ontological priority of the good over all human activity is no longer secure. As in eudaemonism, although in a quite different way, the quest for the good is bent back upon man himself. The good becomes a projection of his own self-realization.

The highest good is now expected from the realization of a rational program. Although this was not Schleiermacher's intention, the spirit of his ethics is similar to the ideology of revolutionary movements in modern history. What is so unsatisfactory about this approach is that definitive programs usually fail to recognize the preliminary character of even the most breathtaking achievements of human action. Therefore revolutionary movements frequently turn conservative, even reactionary, once the immediate goal of the revolution itself is achieved. All too often, the newly established power structure is identified with the highest good. This has been the unhappy experience of our generation with Communism.

The lesson to be learned is of more general significance. Within the reach of human action there is no definitive resolution of the human predicament. At the same time, it is essential and not futile to commit ourselves to the improvement of human life and of the world. In order to keep together both this realistic modesty and this commitment to improvement, a vision of the transcendent is necessary. We do not, to be sure, need any more of a God "out there." Rather we must perceive a transcendence that is engaged in the dynamics of this world. Such a transcendence helps us to gain critical distance from the present and still kindles enthusiasm for the transformation of the present. At the same time, we are reminded of the preliminary state of every possible organization of our world in contrast with the fullness of God's future.

Freedom and Evolutionary Optimism

A commitment to the provisional is essential to Christian faith in the Kingdom of God. To withhold such a commitment because the absolute remains out of reach of human endeavors would mean betraying the Kingdom. And yet it is the special contribution of the eschatological understanding of the Kingdom that it does not allow any particular social program to be mistaken for the Kingdom. The Kingdom reveals itself again and again as still unrealized future that confronts every present and that will confront a, hopefully, better future situation. This futurity of the Kingdom opens ever-new possibilities for action while still denying any human institution the glory of perfection that might warrant its making an absolute claim on the obedience of individuals. The futurity of the Kingdom guards the freedom of the individual from the power of social institutions while, at the same time, enabling the individual to commit himself to the society. Futurity does not mean powerless transcendency but an urgent and imminent future. From such a future spring impulses for relevant criticism and change toward the yet fuller future of freedom, peace, and community life marked by mutual respect and care of its members.

What we have said about the coming Kingdom of God is to be distinguished carefully from any kind of evolutionary optimism, such as that for which the old liberal theology was so rightly blamed. H. Richard Niebuhr, it will be remembered, characterized that superficial optimism in the ironical sentence: "A God without wrath brought men without sin into a kingdom without judgment through the ministrations of a Christ without a cross." Our age has been awakened brutally from euphoric daydreaming about man's inevitable progress. Yet, as sober as we indeed must be, we dare not let the valid criticism of the old liberal assumption blind us to the ethical relevance of the coming Kingdom of God. An equally great danger is that the Kingdom of God should be forgotten in evaluating social structures. In that case Christian thought reverts to the sterile dualism which contrasts this world of sin with the rule of Christ, with the latter usually limited to the Church. This is the familiar formula of Christian conservatism that is rightly condemned for its lack of social responsibility.

A vigorously eschatological understanding of the Kingdom of God can overcome the defects of liberal evolutionism which Niebuhr so cuttingly describes. Such an understanding of the Kingdom does not deafen itself to the wrath of God, nor does it disregard the power of sin in social life. Because the coming Kingdom is not derived from the perspective of human endeavors, but confronts all human activity with the future of God himself, the criticism of the present and the announcement of God's wrath are crucially important. An understanding of reality that is inspired not by the past nor by eternal structures but by the power of the future confronting the present cannot result in a conservative desire to maintain the established order. The very world view or understanding of reality demands that there will be change and calls us to respond creatively to that change. The Christian view of love assumes that the existing world need not face destruction but can hope for salvation, but only if it is transformed. In this process of transforming love there must be criticism of man's obstinate tendencies, of his indolence, and of the structures by which he would protect himself from change. Sin must be uncovered because men are destined for a better future which is promised to them in the imminent Kingdom of God. Criticism of established forms of social life and conflict with the forces of immobilism will always be required. Such conflict once led to the cross of Jesus Christ. The call to take up the cross and follow him must still be issued. And when an individual or a society refuses to change in response to present necessities, then the future will strike them with destruction as God's judgment in history. Those who proclaim the sovereignty of God's coming Kingdom must also be prepared to announce judgment upon a world that rejects the demand for transformation through love.

2

The concrete consequences, the specific courses of action, produced by ethics founded on the coming Kingdom of God cannot be delineated exhaustively or conclusively. God's future expresses itself in a new way for each present. The Kingdom of God is not a detailed program for social change. Yet this understanding of the coming Kingdom does inform and shape the programs required by particular situations. But even those programs most attuned to the coming Kingdom are themselves preliminary. They must be reshaped and replaced as the situation changes. Each specific program and the corresponding criticism of a particular situation constitutes a creative work inspired by the creative power of God's future. It is underivable from past or present as love is underivable and always new because it is always the gift of God's future. Now it may seem that everything said so far about ethics founded upon the coming Kingdom produces only vague generalities. This is far from the case. It is time to examine specific criteria which can be derived from the idea of the coming Kingdom of God and which can illumine the possibilities for human action.

The Dynamic of Love

The fundamental criterion is expressed in the Christian idea of love. Love is no sentimental sensation but the dynamic by which a man is related to the world and, most especially, to his fellowmen. Love is the structure of the divine conversion to the world. Yet love is no impersonal dynamic or structure. Indeed love interprets and underscores the emphatically personal character of human existence. To understand what this means, we must view love in relation to freedom and equality. The notions of freedom and equality have an interpersonal as well as a public or political reference.

Jesus discovered the revelation of God's love in the very fact that the imminent Kingdom of God was announced before its coming in its fullness. That is, God's Kingdom does not come by surprise or as a terror raid that crushes everything that is in its way. No, it is announced beforehand. Men receive the opportunity to open themselves to God's future. In so opening themselves, they can even now find communion with him who is the power that decides the future of all things. In communion with him, they can now anticipate their final significance and essence. The announcement beforehand of the coming Kingdom makes communion with God possible and thus exhibits his love. This communion with the power of the future explains, for instance, Jesus' authority to forgive sins.

Of course communion with God cannot be received by the apathetic, the indifferent, or the inactive. Communion with God is lively participation in his creative love which supports all creatures, grants them their limited duration, and brings them to fulfillment of life by relating them to one another. Since God is the one God of all beings, he can be no respecter of persons. His love is not marked by favoritism toward this individual or that but embraces the whole of mankind and of the world. His love is creating unity, the particular unities which go to make up the individual, and the unities which integrate individuals in society. If we participate in the love of God, we participate in the dynamics that make for unity, especially for the unity by which mankind is joined in the common quest for the highest good. And the highest good for all men, whether they know it or not, is the future of God's Kingdom. If a particular action springs from the spirit of creative love and contributes to individual and social integration, unity, and peace, then that particular action expresses the spirit of God's Kingdom. In pursuing such actions, the life of the individual will be integrated into personal identity and integrity through membership in a communion which is itself related to larger communities and is finally related to the whole of mankind.

The Beloved

Consider the relationship between lover and beloved or the dynamics of friendship. Love, frequently in unexpected ways, creates physical and spiritual integrity in the beloved. True love nurtures wholeness, granting to the beloved the authenticity and independence of his existence. Creative love does not ask the beloved for his dependency but for his personhood. To relate to somebody as a person is no routine thing but an act of faith. Of course, it is all too possible to treat human beings as something less than persons. Their behavior can be calculated as a thing to be exploited for private or public goals. In such cases a man is estimated only according to his normal behavior or proven capability. Not so in the estimate of love. The eyes of love discover something more in a person, something not perceived by all. The eyes of love perceive yet unrealized possibilities.

Ironically, the eyes of love are in this respect similar to the

eyes of fear and suspicion. Unrealized possibilities are also perceived by the person who feels he must guard himself against
another person. But respect for the enemy or suspicion of another person is usually confined to the other's potential abilities. Respect and suspicion seldom include a sense of solidarity, of identity, with the other. Love, on the other hand, envisions in the beloved the destiny of his life and the promise
of life's fulfillment. Love views the beloved with the eyes of
God. Yet love too respects the beloved. He anticipates that the
potential will be realized through the other person's own decision and effort. Love can support, but it does not seek to control, the struggle toward realization.

This loving respect for the other person, this concentration
on the other person's self-determination has a theological rationale. The respect for the identity of the beloved is required
by the immediacy of each individual in his personal destination
to God. Personal immediacy to God precludes interference by
others in the mystery of one's own personal decision. Love
sometimes must anticipate the potential perfection of the other
person in the eyes of God when such anticipation seems to be
defied by the facts; the facts of the other's ordinarily poor performance or of tragic circumstances which cripple the possibilities of life. At such times it is more difficult to respect the
mystery of personal decision. But it is the way of love to liberate the beloved to his freedom. All respect for personal freedom and self-determination, unless it proceeds from mere awe
or dread, includes an element of love.

Yet the destiny of lover and beloved is not a purely private
matter; love calls for more than mutual respect of individual
identities. Genuine respect arising from love includes an ultimate sense of human solidarity with the other person. His possibilities for fulfillment in the presence of God cannot be completely foreign to me. Our hope is a common hope, human
destiny is the same for all humanity, although realized in myriad ways. Thus not freedom alone but freedom and equality
mark all human relations. This equality is asserted in the face
of enormous differences in terms of particular possibilities, individual vocations, and social status. To accept somebody as a

person means conceding to him an ultimate equality with myself in the human vocation. The recognition of equality demands expression in opportunities for each person to achieve a life-style of human dignity, to develop individual gifts, to make his distinctive contribution to his own group and, beyond that, to mankind.

So love desires personal integrity and personal integrity requires freedom and equality. The realizations and frustrations of love can be studied in the history of marriage and of relations between the sexes as well as of society and political life. In none of these areas is freedom and equality realized in any ultimate way. With regard to society, it is one of the tasks of ethical criticism to uncover the limits of the respective realizations of freedom and equality and to project new possibilities for the institutionalizing of their higher forms.

Equality in Destiny

It has not always been self-evident that Christian love implies the liberation of fellowmen to freedom and equality. In the New Testament the idea of freedom is to mark the new life of the believer, but it took a long historical development for the implications of this insight to break through. The Christian idea of freedom and equality cannot be equated with the idea present in Stoic philosophy. Yet in the political history of the West there was a merger of the two, a merger that has had some unfortunate consequences. The Stoic understanding was that originally all men were free and equal but their nature was corrupted by their own shortcomings, by the vices of social life. The idea is fraught with problems. It takes little analytical skill to look around and see that men are neither free nor equal. If they were free and equal by nature, this nature should be discoverable somewhere beneath the surface of social corruptions. But quests for the "natural" man, to say nothing of the natural mankind of freedom and equality, are futile. Instead we discover real and great differences in circumstances, in talents and character as well as in merit and honor. It would be unjust to disregard what excels as it would be cruel to demand equal results from persons of unequal abilities.

Not the present reality nor some mythical origin, but the final destiny of man is free and equal. The Christian, through faith in Jesus the Christ, participates even now in this final destiny. One must not confuse this reality of faith with the empirical condition of human life at our present moment of social history. But the Christian faith can inspire a change and sustain the struggle for new formations of social life.

Seventeenth-century Christians arriving in America found the courage to build even their political life on the premises of freedom and equality. They embraced freedom and equality in their faith and intended to incarnate it in their social structures. Freedom and equality were assumed not simply as facts but as the values shaping the goal of social enterprise. The goal was to be realized by making men *more and more* free and equal, not by reducing everyone to some average level but by giving everyone opportunity to realize his highest potential. This means that more support must be provided for the underprivileged so that their opportunity may be genuinely equal. This " compensation " to the underprivileged moves, at least theoretically, beyond the formalistic notion of equality in Western democracy, a notion that came under vigorous attack from the Marxist critique. Formal freedom and equality that consists only of legal provisions and rights can indeed be meaningless for people who have no opportunity to take advantage of their rights. To increase real freedom and equality, not merely to provide legal guarantees for formal freedom and equality, is the ongoing task of democratic societies.

Society and the Individual

Where freedom and equality have become the basis of political life, the individual is the purpose of society. The state is made for man, not man for the state. The history of constitutional government demonstrates the necessity of limiting the extent and use of political power. The idea that individuals represent the purpose of the society is basic to the concept of self-government. The history of modern democratic thought is inexplicable without reference to the notions of self-government and of the sovereignty of the people. Yet, if understood literally, the idea of self-government is an illusion. Nowhere does the entire body of individuals constitute the government; indeed if the government were composed of everyone, there would be no government at all. The very concept of government assumes that there is in some sense a body of the governed. Certainly, the simple fact that a government is dependent upon regular elections does not mean that there is self-government. It is sometimes suggested that, even if it is not literally accurate, we ought to hold on to the concept of self-government as an ideal. But maintaining the notion of self-government is dangerous because it tends to disguise the real power structure that prevails in a society. It is more honest and politically helpful for the people to have a clear understanding of the individuals and interests that actually wield power. The myth of self-government inhibits the people in demanding accountability from the power structures in the society.

There should be no government without the consent of the majority of the people. Ruling circles are always built upon minorities, sometimes very slim minorities at that. But their exercise of political power should be conditioned, as it is in democratic societies, not only by their ability to convince the majority of the people but by their ability to convince the majority in open contest with candidates and programs that represent a real alternative. Such democratic convincing must rely more on argumentation than on propaganda. Of course every party and cause falls prey to the temptation to use propaganda. But this must always be viewed as a failure of democratic process and a temptation to be resisted vigorously, for there is no doubt that human dignity is disdained by those who resort to persuasive means other than the argumentation that calls for decision.

The Commonweal

Democracy is also polluted when governments and parties bribe their constituents, buying off the more powerful elements in the society. Too often the public wealth is dissipated in an attempt to satisfy the narrow interests of pressure groups, whose votes a party thinks it dare not lose. The more difficult and creative task is to inspire the majority of the people toward the achievement of the commonweal. Politicians must have the courage to recognize the difference between the wishes of the people, even of a majority of the people, and the common good.

The tension between the interests of pressure groups and the commonweal can be understood as a tension between the sovereignty of the people and the Kingdom of God. In its relevance to a particular social situation, the Kingdom of God is manifest in the common good. Ancient democracy failed because, in this tension, the endeavor to please the majority became the preoccupation of rival groupings, and the commonweal was neglected. It is by no means certain that modern democracy will escape this fate. The commonweal will thrive in a society only where a universal spirit unites the individuals and leads them beyond their narrow self-interests. And, of course, this cannot be achieved unless such a people knows to live in peace with the rest of the world. Only where the commonweal thrives can freedom and equality of the individuals grow and only there can liberal institutions survive. The commonweal, the manifestation of God's sovereignty, must be elevated above the people's sovereignty. Sovereignty of the people can only be sustained where the commonweal is esteemed.

It is the task of public opinion to guard the priority of the commonweal in the process of political discussion and action. In this connection we must understand the contribution of the Christian proclamation. The Christian proclamation points to the imminent Kingdom of God by advocating the priority of the commonweal over all conflicting claims. This proclamation should prove itself to be a moral center in the formation of public opinion.

But what is the commonweal? Again we must see that the idea of the Kingdom of God does not refer only or even primarily to the individual personality. Indeed, in the original hope for God's Kingdom, as in the Old Testament, the great terms are peace and justice, distinctly social realities. In the message of Jesus, to be sure, the proclamation of the Kingdom is addressed to each individual and calls for personal decision. But the social dimension is far from lost. The very decision of the individual points to a communal hope. At stake is whether or not the individual will be part of the new society of the children of God. The personal decision cannot be separated from the communal promise of God's love manifest in the peace and justice that is to exist within a given society and is to order relationships among societies.

What Makes for Peace

We must ask more precisely about the nature and the conditions of peace. Peace is premised upon mutual acknowledgment. Mutual acknowledgment, as we have seen, is essential to the closest personal community. It is equally essential to peace in international relations. The process of mutual acknowledgment is, furthermore, constitutive for the idea of justice. Through this argumentation, it becomes clear that there is a close relationship between peace and justice, on the one hand, and freedom and equality on the other.

Peace is a provisional state of justice that is mutually acknowledged by the several parties concerned. Since the state of justice is always provisional, peace is always " for the time being." There simply is no definitive measure to tell us what is just for all times and in all situations. In assuming such a definitive measure, the Greeks were wrong. Justice is realized, more or less, for a shorter or longer period of time, in a social process. It requires an element of love in the acknowledgment of conflicts and in the determination of conditions conducive to a state of peace, that is, to a state based on new forms of mutual agreement, or of justice. There is an element of love in this process because it is never explained exhaustively merely by reference to the pressures and dreads between the conflicting groups. There is always that moment in which love overcomes fear. To the degree that the power of love is active in the emerging consensus, there will be a movement toward fuller realization of freedom and equality for both sides in the conflict.

Just the recognition of conflict is a beginning toward peace.

Without a mutual acknowledgment of differences there can be no effort to resolve the differences. And of course this assumes a mutual recognition, including diplomatic recognition, of the very existence of the parties. Such recognition is at the basis of whatever we might hope for in terms of world peace. The differences between societies must be respected within the context of common responsibilities for a wider community of nations and of all mankind. Mutual respect, implying the recognition of each other's freedom and, at least to some extent, of each other's equality, is pointedly relevant also to the development of international relations.

An old and good principle of Christian political ethics is that the unity of mankind corresponds to the universality of the one God. There can be no peace unless the community of mankind is given priority over national interests. Certainly, any attempt in our day to realize the unity of mankind by imposing the uniformity of an empire must be regarded as utopian and frightening. Perhaps the imperial model never was a viable way to achieve unity. In any case, it is not viable today. The peace of mankind can be achieved only by a process of intensified and mutual acknowledgment of different national concerns and cultural styles. In such acknowledgment it is possible to anticipate a provisional realization of the eschatological unity of mankind, a unity for which we must yet wait and work.

The emergence of myriad needs and desires, frequently in competition and conflict with one another, witness to the provisionality of our present realization of the coming Kingdom. We ought not be surprised by continuing conflicts within and between societies. In our preliminary moment of history, antagonisms are indispensable for bringing present forms under criticism and for pointing to new possibilities for the reordering of the human community. Conflict gives birth to positive values and the birth pangs are the price to be paid. It is true that conflict can lead to mutual destruction. This is the danger when men attempt to hasten the unity of the Kingdom by imposing uniformity and destroying the pluralism of human existence. The unity we seek does indeed lead beyond the antagonisms resulting from an immoderate pluralism. But this unity leads us through processes of mutual acknowledgment and of cooperation between opposing groups. In all our reflection about both unity and pluralism, we recall that our point of view is preliminary. The preliminary nature of our present and of our present projections for the future is at the heart of an ethics conditioned on the coming Kingdom of God.

Intuitions of the Ultimate

Jesus himself was only a forerunner. He revealed the redeeming love of God precisely as the forerunner and herald of God's still imminent Kingdom. His message was a preliminary and precisely in that way he participated in and revealed the ultimate reality, the love of God. To love the preliminary is no little thing. Christians are surely right to call for devotion to Jesus. He who despises the preliminary because he waits for the ultimate will not be able to recognize the ultimate in its coming. The history of modern revolutions illustrates the fatal flaw in living so exclusively for the future that all cherishing and celebrating of the present are precluded. In the name of the future the values of past and present are disdained and destroyed. The mediocre realities of our present, although they have no ultimate claim on us, are to be nurtured for the intuitions of the ultimate which they possess. To be converted to the world means to be converted to the present in the hope of fulfillment.

Hope for the coming Kingdom knows that ultimate fulfillment is beyond human powers to effect. Yet, far from being condemned to inactivity, we are inspired to prepare this present for the future. Such preparation is the work of hope carried out by love. Conscious of the preliminary character of his achievements, the man of hope is open to more promising answers to the problems that claim his energy. Thus he is opened beyond himself to the future of God's Kingdom.

CHAPTER IV

Appearance as the Arrival of the Future

Ambiguities of language often indicate a problematic subject matter. That is the case with the word " appear " (*erscheinen*). When I say that an acquaintance (or someone with whom I was previously unacquainted) "appeared" to me, in order to speak with me, the meaning is: he came to me, he showed up in my habitat, perhaps at my home. He did not only seem (*scheinen*) to be there; he really was there. When something appears to us, it does not only seem to be with us, it actually is present. Appearance and existence are here very closely connected. But on the other hand, my acquaintance still exists even when he does not appear to me. Whether that would still be true if he appeared nowhere — whether my acquaintance would then still exist — that is, of course, questionable. But that question I will set aside. In any case, the existence of my acquaintance is not the same as his appearing to *me*. Thus, we differentiate between what something is in and for itself (or also for others) and the way it appears to and for us. This distinction is already present in the word " appear." What appears to me is precisely that which is, in and for itself, something more than it is as it presently appears to me. In this sense, according to Kant, the idea of appearance points back to a being-in-itself which is different from the appearance, since it would be nonsense to say that there is appearance without there being something to appear.[1] What is meant is not only that appearance has a concrete form. Rather, the con-

cept of appearance implies that in it something manifests itself which is something more than that part of it which appears. The ambiguity of the word appearance is thus based on
the relation of appearance to being. On the one hand, appearing and existence mean the same thing. But on the other hand,
appearance, taken literally, points to a being transcending it.
How are these two sides of the word's meaning to be united?
Or do they fall totally asunder, so that the unity of the word
connecting the two is only an insignificant coincidence?

1

With this question we turn to the history of thought about
appearance. Since Parmenides at the latest, and especially under the powerful influence of Plato, the tendency to separate
appearance and being has been dominant. The world of appearance, of *doxa,* is considered a mixture of being and non-
being, of a lesser order than the being which exists in itself.
In Platonism this latter being is depicted as the being of the
ideas, which is reflected only imperfectly in the appearances
and which remains inaccessible to sense perception, although
the understanding grasps it. This being is held to exist in itself, eternally and unchangeably; the appearances in which it
is reflected add nothing to it. Of course, it must be mentioned
that this interpretation, which was expressed most decisively
by Plato himself in the *Phaedo* and the *Republic,* does not ex-
haust the full profundity of his thought about the idea. Originally, the appearance was included in the idea as the perceived form, as especially Julius Stenzel has shown; the idea
is precisely the form shining through *in* the appearance, so
that, for example, the idea of beauty is experienced in what is
beautifully shaped. From such a point of departure the complete separation of the idea from its appearance could only be
a fringe possibility for Plato. And he himself showed it to be
untenable in his *Parmenides:* If idea and appearance are separated from each other, then another idea is needed to account
for the relatedness of the first two. But if this new idea as such
is again separated from those things (idea and appearance) for

whose similarity it is supposed to account, then a further idea is required, etc.[2] The separation between idea and appearance, the divorce so strongly attacked by Aristotle, was recognized by Plato himself to be untenable. Of course, that Plato overcame it can hardly be asserted. The influence upon him of the Eleatic understanding of being seems to have been too strong for that, especially the notion that true being, in its immutability, *needs* nothing beyond itself for its being.[3] Thus, for the idea, understood as true being, the relation to the appearance must be a matter of indifference, and in this self-sufficiency of the idea the separation from its appearances continues to exist. Even Aristotle, as his notion of substance shows, was not able completely to escape the suggestion of the Eleatic understanding of being. So it becomes understandable that the separation of true being from its appearance, the precedence of self-sufficient ideas or substances reposing in themselves over the phenomenal reality of sense experience, remained a dominant motif in the history of thought whenever the notion of appearance became thematic.

Against this background it was of great significance when the relation between essence and appearance came to be recognized as reciprocal. In order to find the reciprocity of this relationship explicitly formulated, we must take a broad leap over the whole history of the relation of essence and appearance. We find it so formulated by Hegel. According to him, the relation is such that the appearance not only points back to the essence appearing in it as to its truth, the reverse is also true: "Essence *must* appear. Seeming (*das Scheinen*) is the definiteness, through which essence is not mere being, but essence, and fully developed seeming is appearance. Essence is thus not behind or beyond appearance, but existence is appearance by virtue of the fact that it is essence which exists."[4] To understand fully Hegel's statement here we would have to go into the changes that the concept of essence had undergone from Plato's notion of true being and Aristotle's category of *ousia* down to Hegel. Only out of the dissolution of the Aristotelian concept of substance could the strange situation become more understandable, that in Hegel's statement essence is set over against being, rather than itself being directly depicted as true being. Be that as it may, the statement that essence must appear is still intended by Hegel in the sense of an ontological precedence of essence over its appearance, even if the essence first comes into view by going behind the world of being into its ground, since being is now characterized as appearance of a ground that differs from it, i.e., the essence. Appearance thereby presents itself as mere reflection, as self-alienation of the essence, which, in the process of Hegel's logic, is to be more precisely defined as concept and idea. Since the Hegelian idea is thought of as timeless, logical structure — being therein similar to the timeless being of Parmenides — appearance in Hegel's philosophy (contrary to his insight into the reciprocity of the relation of essence and appearance) is again reduced to the status of the nonessential. Instead of — as Hegel asserted — the idea existing only in the appearances, it in fact finds in the appearances of religion or history merely subsequent illustrations of its fixed, logical structure.

The separtion of being (or essence) and appearance can then evidently be avoided only if one approaches being and essence by beginning with appearance even more decisively than Hegel himself did. Kant offers a beginning in this direction with his thesis that all functioning of the understanding is related to appearance. However, since he presupposed the traditional opposition of the thing in itself and the appearance, Kant meant to express with this thesis the fundamental limitation of all human knowing. Nevertheless, his thesis could lead to thinking of appearanceness as the fundamental characteristic of being itself. To my knowledge, Heinrich Barth has taken this course more consistently than anyone else. Barth allows being in the sense of subsistence only to appearance [5] and rejects every "reduction of the appearance to non-appearing being-in-itself." [6] Finally, he understands the "something" that appears, and apart from which (according to Kant) appearance cannot be thought, as the eidetic content in the act of appearing itself, which forms the theme of the *interpretation* of the appearance. The statement that the meaning of the appearance (which is, in its actuality and contingency, already presupposed) is expressed in the *eidos*,[7] reverses the traditional interpretation of the relation of *eidos* and appearance. The appearing as existence takes priority over all notions of essence. Barth's understanding of appearance accordingly reveals itself as bound up with the post-Hegelian situation, in which the priority of " being-there," of existence, over against all "whatness," all eidetic structures, has been repeatedly affirmed. When it is not limited to anthropology, this priority agrees, albeit remotely, with the Anglo-Saxon tradition of empiricism. Over against modes of thought that take what exists in its pure facticity as the point of departure, Barth's orientation in terms of phenomena, his view of existence as what appears,[8] proves itself superior by the fact that the notion of appearing simultaneously comprehends both the act of coming-into-appearance and the " something " that appears, thus the eidetic or essential element.

Heinrich Barth's new interpretation of the notion of appearance opens the way for the contingency of events, for the historicity of all experience, insofar as its occurrence is always presupposed in the interpretation of its content. Nevertheless, the interpretation of the contingent appearances is not limited to the sphere of events, but goes beyond it. Interpretation can take place only by going beyond the event that gives rise to the interpretation. Insofar as this is true, the " something " that appears cannot be thought of as totally exhausted in the act of appearing. It is precisely and only for this reason that the characterization of the existing as *appearance* can be justified. In going beyond the event in the process of its interpretation, a difference arises anew (and in a new sense) between appearance and being, between appearance and essence.

This going beyond the appearance in its interpretation can be clarified by reference to very old themes, which are, not accidentally of course, also Socratic themes: In saying *what* appears in the individual appearance, a something is always named that appears not only here, but elsewhere as well. By virtue of this generality (however it is to be interpreted), the *eidos* transcends the individual appearance in which it is encountered.

Connected with the possibility of manifold appearances of one and the same *eidos* is the fact that it exhausts itself in none of its appearances. There always remain other ways in which " the same " *eidos* could appear. One could draw from this the completely unplatonic consequence that the *eidos* contains in itself an element of indeterminacy beyond what can be known of it from its appearance or from a plurality of such appearances. Yet, in any case (and this is only the other side of the same thing), the individual appearance always presents itself as only a partial realization of the possibilities of the *eidos* appearing in it. The work of art seems to be an exception to this rule. In the harmony of part and whole that exists in the work of art, the difference between essence and appearance is, in a certain sense, overcome. This is the basis of the perfection of the work of art. But in everyday reality such harmony is not found. Here the multiplicity of appearances is the sign of the imperfection of each individual one.

So far we have seen that neither the separation of true being and appearance nor the thesis of their identity can be maintained without turning into the respective opposite. From the *separation* of idea and appearance, or essence and appearance, we are directed to the fact that they belong together. But with the assertion of the identity of the appearance and the existence of the appearing something, the difference between appearance and essence breaks out anew, because the interpretation of that something which appears unavoidably goes beyond the event of its isolated appearance. Now that the theses of the separation and of the identity of appearance and true being have both been shown to be one-sided, the question is raised as to whether the unity of the identity and nonidentity of appearance and being is accessible to a more penetrating description.

2

The theologian may be excused for introducing a theological example at this place in the train of thought. This is not done to silence the intellectual question with an authoritative answer. Rather, the example may directly contribute to a better understanding of the difference and the unity of appearance and that which appears.

The well-known and controversial problem of the relation of the futurity and presence of the Reign of God in the ministry of Jesus seems to me to be relevant for illuminating the unity and difference of appearance and that which appears. In the oldest layers of the New Testament traditions of Jesus are sayings that speak of the presence of the Reign of God in the ministry of Jesus. These stand alongside sayings that differentiate the Reign of God as something future from the present ministry of Jesus. Whether and how both groups of sayings are to be reconciled is today a major exegetical question. I myself find most convincing the arguments of those exegetes who do not opt in favor of one of the two sides, and do not unravel the difficulties by eliminating one group of opposing sayings as unauthentic, but rather seek the uniqueness of the message of Jesus precisely in this juxtaposition of seemingly opposing sayings. But how is such juxtaposition to be understood? In the sense of a future extension and completion of that which has broken in in the present? I prefer the opposite view: that in the ministry of Jesus the futurity of the Reign of God became a power determining the present. For Jesus, the traditional Jewish expectation of the coming Reign of God on earth became the decisive and all-encompassing content of ones relation to God, since the coming Reign of God had to do with the coming of God himself. Thus, obedience to God, with the complete exclusiveness of the Jewish understanding of God, became turning to the future of the Reign of God. But wherever that occurs, there God already reigns unconditionally in the present, and such presence of the Reign of God does not conflict with its futurity but is derived from it and is itself only the anticipatory glimmer of its coming. Accordingly, in Jesus' ministry, in his call to seek the Kingdom of God, the coming Reign of God has already appeared, without ceasing to be differentiated from the presentness of such an appearance. The divine confirmation of this matter, which came to Jesus' disciples through the Easter appearances, was the basis for the later Christian mode of expression, that God himself had uniquely and definitively appeared in Jesus without the difference between Jesus and God himself being thereby dissolved. The later Christological doctrine speaks appropriately of the deity of Jesus, which nevertheless, as that of the " Son," remains different from that of the Father. This, in the final analysis, is still a matter of the interpretation of the " appearance " of God, of the presence of his Reign, in the ministry of Jesus. The difference of the Son from the Father, to which the Christological doctrine holds fast, corresponds to the continuing difference in the message of Jesus between the futurity of the Reign of God and its presence in Jesus' ministry. And just as the future, precisely in its abiding difference from the present, is the basis for the present efficacy of God's Reign (and thus for its entrance into the present), so is the deity of Jesus himself, as that of the " Son," based precisely on Jesus' holding fast to the difference between God the Father and himself. Jesus did not raise the claim of divine authority for his own person — as his opponents evidently misunderstood him. Rather, he subjected himself totally to something different from himself, which he called " the Father," to God's coming Reign; only so was the coming Reign of God — God himself — already present in him. The difference between Jesus' present and the Father's future was ever and again actualized in the surrender of the man Jesus to the coming Reign of God that he proclaimed, insofar as it was the future of another. Jesus pointed away from himself; therefore, the interpretation of that which appeared in him must go beyond the appearance of Jesus, to God, whom his message concerned. For this reason any mixing of the divine and human in the event of the appearance of God in this man is in error. And yet, precisely in Jesus' *pointing* away from himself to God's future did this future as such become present in and through him. The appearance of God in this man, which transcends his finite existence, means, just because of this, an existence of God in him, a oneness of God with him. The coming-to-appearance of God in Jesus has thereby a different meaning from the epiphanies of gods in human or animal form, of which we hear, e.g., in the history of

Greek religion. There, any particular form of the appearance, being replaceable, remains external to the essence of the deity, just as in Plato or Parmenides, its appearance remains nonessential to true being.[9] In the ministry of Jesus, on the contrary, the God of Israel, the future of his Reign, comes definitively to appearance once. He manifested himself in this single event conclusively and for all time, and just for this reason only once. This is how the later ecclesiastical doctrine of the incarnation expressed the matter, over against all Hellenistic notions of an epiphany. The finality of Jesus' ministry is based on its eschatological character, on the fact that through it the ultimate future of God's Reign becomes determinative of the present and therefore becomes present. Appearance and essential presence are here one. Is not this character of the appearance of God in Jesus — as opposed to the different religio-historical background of the Platonic-Parmenidean relation between appearance and true being — also relevant for considering the problem of appearance in general?

Of course, little would be gained if without further ado we tried to abstract a general concept of appearance from the way in which God came to appearance in Jesus of Nazareth. In so proceeding one would merely arrive at theological postulates for which he could, at most, try to claim general validity. We would rather ask whether our theological example throws light on certain, perhaps otherwise hidden, sides of the general philosophical problem of appearance. The pursuit of this question can be sufficiently motivated by the fact that in Christian reflection on the appearance of God in Jesus of Nazareth the two elements are united which have again and again broken apart in philosophical reflection, although they are both suggested when appearance is discussed, i.e., the effective presence of what appears in the appearance, and its transcendence of the individual appearance. In the idea of the revelation of God in Jesus of Nazareth both are combined: God is completely and conclusively present in this individual man, and yet God remains different from him; in fact, it is just as the One who is different from Jesus that God is in him. We have seen that this unity of the seemingly mutually exclusive ele-

ments is understandable (and grounded) in the way that God's
Reign is still future in relation to the ministry and message of
Jesus and yet, as future, is present in it. Does the connection
of identity and difference in the relation of being (or essence)
and appearance have something to do with the temporality of
this relation? And does that which appears in the appearance
thereby present itself in the mode of futurity?

3

If we look at the beginnings of Greek philosophizing, it can
well be said that Heinrich Barth has rightly described the
theme of appearance as already the theme of the Ionian philosophers of nature. This judgment seems to me to be confirmed precisely through the structure of the quest for the
archē, in which Heinrich Barth found the point of departure
for the ontological " reduction " of appearance to semblance
(*Schein*).[10] In going beyond the immediately experienced multiplicity in the quest for its common ground, all that is achieved
at first is that the element of difference between appearance
and appearing essence, which is constitutive for the appearance as such, receives its due. That things " are " different
" fundamentally " (i.e., in their ground) in contrast to what
they " seem " to be — is this not the basic conviction of every
view that experiences reality as appearance, as opposed to a
superficial empiricism content with what is immediately ob-
servable? But this conviction of fundamental difference is not
enough to distinguish the Ionian thinkers from the experience
of existence that found its expression in myth. For the mythical intuition also saw something deeper in that which is immediately visible. The intuitive certainty of this vision, which
grasps precisely in the phenomenon what the things " fundamentally " are, did not, of course, seem to the Ionian philosophers of nature to be a possibility. What the true nature of
the " ground " is had become questionable. Different answers
were given. By becoming questionable the phenomena had already lost their transparency to their deeper ground. Insofar
as the philosophical answers now named the one ground, to

which, however, the phenomena are not transparent, the "possibility of a devaluation of the appearance" arose.[11] It is thus implicitly presupposed that the ground has always been there, so that the phenomena really — if they were not deceptive semblance — would have to set the viewer free to see through them to the ground present in them. Parmenides is the first to affirm the present givenness of the ground in a reflective way, in that the "is," being absolutely self-identical and unconditionally present, is accorded the function of the *archē*, as the common and unifying element of everything that is.[12] Since the "is" is absolutely self-identical and one, and as such is present, everything manifold and changeable becomes deceptive semblance. This devaluation of the phenomena into mere semblance does not yet follow from the difference of the ground from the phenomena in which it appears, but only from the situation where the phenomena no longer show what they already are "fundamentally." When "in ground" the only true being is already present, then the phenomena, in their difference from the ground, can only be considered deceptive concealment.

In Parmenides, therefore, the future has no place in the understanding of appearance. It is different with the second root of the classical philosophy of appearance, which confronts us in Plato. The Platonic idea points, on the one hand, back to the Parmenidean understanding of being, but its other and original root lies in the Socratic quest for the good in the life of the *polis*, and thus for ἀρετή, the true virtue, which knows the good and the useful, and acts accordingly. An element of futurity is contained in the notion of the good. Insofar as everyone strives for the good and the useful, as is said in the *Gorgias*, it is clear that no one already finds himself in its possession; rather, he hopes to attain unto it. Thus, in the essence of the good, as that which is striven for, there is something future. This is confirmed by the famous Platonic expression in the *Republic* that the good is to be thought of as transcending what exists (ἐπέκεινα τῆς οὐσίας). Of course, the transcendence of the good is not there based on the fact that striving is a going beyond that which is presently given, but on the transcendence of the cause (the ideas as true being) over that which is caused by it. But causality itself ($\alpha\dot{\iota}\tau\dot{\iota}\alpha$) is, for Plato, connected with striving.

Now if we, with Julius Stenzel, understand the Platonic idea as the full form of the goodness and virtue of the things in question, which it "imitatively" strives to attain, then it is clear that the Platonic understanding of the relation of idea and appearance includes, from its Socratic background, a relation to the future. And this is not a relation of visible things to just any sort of future, but to their essential future, to their "good." The idea of the good might then perhaps be understood in a precise sense as the "idea of the ideas," that is, it in sum has as its content that which constitutes every idea as idea. Already the Socrates of the Platonic *Phaedo* could say, not only of the society, but also of the whole cosmos, that "the good and useful is that which connects and holds together" and thus fulfills the *archē*'s function of unifying the many.

In Plato's conception of the idea, of course, the Socratic motif of the good clashes with the Parmenidean conception of true being. Since the ideas are understood in the Eleatic sense as true being, the motif of futurity, which is present in the Socratic striving for the good, cannot lead to a new understanding of being. It is only as presently at hand that the Platonic ideas form that world of true being behind the real world which has so often been a source of reproach against Platonism. And it is with this world behind the real world that the notorious difficulties are introduced into the question of how the appearances can then participate in the ideas. For the original "ethical" question concerning the good there were no such difficulties: the good as the sought after, essential future was just as much connected to present things as it was different from them. Insofar as the good as idea could be viewed in what was present, the arrival of its essential future was therein experienced.

To a certain extent the thought of Aristotle seems in our questions, as in so many others, to be a renaissance of the Socratic mode of thought. In the Aristotelian connection of *eidos* and *telos,* the Socratic striving for the good (and the futuristic element implied therein) finds a new ontological formulation. The essence of a thing, its *eidos*, is the goal of its movement — at least of its natural, unforced movement. Thus, the yet unattained goal is present in an anticipatory way in the moved as entelechy, and this indwelling of the goal effects the movement toward the goal. For Aristotle, this was explicitly connected with the Socratic question about the good: " According to our doctrine, then," he says in the first book of the *Physics*, " there is, on the one side, something divine, good, desirable; on the other side, the opposite (privation, formlessness); and in between, something which by nature strives for the good."

The futurism of this Aristotelian analysis of movement is neutralized, however, by two notions. The first is the notion of self-movement, already conceived of by the later Plato. According to this doctrine the entelechy is not the anticipation of the *not yet* attained goal, but is the already present (*vorhanden*) germ, out of which the goal unfolds itself. This inner teleology, which reverses the relation of present and future, has robbed evolutionary thought until our day of the possibility of seeing what is new in each event as something really new. Even more decisive for Aristotle himself is the notion expressed in his *Metaphysics* that the goal of the movement, in order to be able to cause the movement, must already be somewhere. But if the movement brings forth nothing except what is already actual somewhere else, then nothing new can arise. Also, for Aristotle the realm of forms is timeless, i.e., unlimited presence. Thus, in Aristotle the Eleatic understanding of being prevailed once again. From this followed the Aristotelian downgrading of individual and contingent entities, which were not seen as coming from the future, but only negatively as nonessential. The Christian Aristotelianism of the Middle Ages saw itself driven to a re-evaluation here, since the Christian doctrine of creation ascribes to God the bringing forth of something new. Here the contingency of the occurrence was positively understood as expressive of the freedom of the Creator. But the coherence of contingency with an ontological priority of the future was not reflected upon even

here, so that in the Christian scholastics the Aristotelian metaphysics of form remained as an unrecognized and unconquered
alien element.

Modern philosophy has dissolved the Aristotelian metaphysics of substantial forms, and dissolved it, indeed, into appearance. However, since the primary qualities (the spatial body)
as well as the secondary qualities of sense perception, and finally (in Kant) the substance itself, disappeared into a general relativity, that which appears "receded" from the horizon
of modern philosophy. Philosophy no longer succeeded in
thinking of what appears independently of the way in which it
appears. So only human experience, as the place of the appearing itself, remained to determine the content of what appears.
When this is rightly reflected upon, the origin of appearance
can no longer be specified as a presently existing being. But
this did not lead to thinking of appearance in its contingency
as the happening of that which is future (*des Zukünftigen*).
Instead, Kant construed the appearing content to be conditioned through the forms of our faculty of knowledge. In their
synthetic nature, these forms portray constructions of the productive power of imagination, which finds in experience what
is not really present to be perceived in the sensibly given, yet
characterizes what appears in the sensibly given. Thus, the
productive imagination goes beyond what is primarily given
in experience. But in thus going beyond, where does it go?
If we raise this question in view of the way that modern subjectivity is related to its world in general, which is, among
other things, represented by Kant's productive imagination, is
it not then to be said that the subjectivity goes beyond the
given and alters it in that it makes *itself* into the future of its
world, be it through technology or by the constructions of the
imagination? Do we not then have to understand the synthetic
constructions of the productive imagination (if we set aside
Kant's hypothesis of an unchanging structure of human experience) as *anticipations* of the essential future of what is
given in appearance? Is it not only with this presupposition
that we can possibly understand the miracle of the correspondence to objective reality and of the realizability of spontane-

ous human constructions? Inversely, if appearance were to be understood as something that happens out of the essential future of that which appears, then its interpretation with reference to *that which appears* would only be possible by an anticipation of the future, as this anticipation characterizes the creative subjectivity of the imagination. (It may be mentioned in passing that such anticipation remains in itself ambiguous, because it can misrepresent the essential future of the appearing reality as well as grasp it.)

4

I must now interrupt this line of thought in the midst of such open questions and summarize. In the section above we have dealt with the question of whether the appearing reality is to be understood more as the appearance of something that always is or as the arrival of what is future. Both ways have their religio-historical backgrounds: the one coming from myth's orientation to primal time and the archetypical, the other from being grasped by an eschatological future. The first way is a well-beaten path and has been impressed on all our familiar habits of thought. The second way has until now been hardly considered. And yet, the beginnings of it are shown even in classical statements of the traditional understanding of being. There is much to be said in favor of orienting philosophical thinking to that which always is. Above all, one may point to the possibility of forming general concepts and of making general structural statements that can be applied to the most diverse individuals and to changing situations. And yet, against this view is the truth that such a position, which sees what appears in the appearance only as a timeless universal, will inevitably underestimate or totally fail to recognize the importance for our experience of reality, of the contingently new, of the individual, and of time. Accordingly, it seems more appropriate to consider the universal as a human construction, which indeed proves itself useful by its ability to grasp a reality that is probably of quite another character, since it is conditioned by contingency and time.

The real basis of the universality of the abstractions we construct is perhaps to be sought in *repetition*, which plays such a large role in all events. Innumerable new events "repeat" earlier ones, although they always bring forth something new. The element of change remains unobservable in the overwhelming majority of events; thus, from a sufficiently broad perspective, one can speak of a repetition of *the same* structures in an indefinite multiplicity of events. And from this can arise the conception of that which is ever the same, of the eternal presence of the *eidos*. This interpretation is particularly suggestive because man, by means of such constructions, asserts himself over against the unfathomable number of contingent events. Is not man seeking an absolute confirmation of himself in the apotheosis of what always is? But, in reality, do not men succeed in producing such constructions, which must be made ever-anew, only by exposing themselves to the uncertainty that lies in the contingent experience of reality and in the contingency even of one's own constructing? Must not man endure this lack of security, since he himself does not yet live in the final future, but rather is ever and again surprised by what comes upon him from the future? Eternal presence could be the experience only of what is itself the final future.

Perhaps even the phenomenon of repetition can be approached in terms of the arrival of what is future: The contingently new becomes present event by taking up into itself, or by repeating, the existing situation, insofar as it is not able to transform it into a new synthesis. This is the basic idea of Alfred North Whitehead's philosophy of nature. The contingency of the event apparently includes an element of faithfulness. As is well known, the first discussion of repetition in connection with the idea of faithfulness was Kierkegaard's treatment of it in the human realm. But perhaps this notion has a wider significance. The arrival of what is future may be thought through to its conclusion only with the idea of repetition (which does not exclude the new), in the sense that in it the future *has* arrived in a *permanent* present.

If we reflect once more upon our theological example, upon the *definitive meaning* of the *appearance* of God's future in

Jesus of Nazareth, in which God's *love* is revealed, then perhaps this can be said: The future *wills* to become present; it tends toward its arrival in a permanent present.

NOTES TO CHAPTER IV

1. Kant, *Critique of Pure Reason,* Preface to Second Edition.

2. *Parmenides,* 132 (the idea of greatness and of great things), 133.

3. Diels, *Fragment,* 8, 33.

4. Hegel, *Enzyklopädie,* 131.

5. Heinrich Barth, *Philosophie der Erscheinung,* II, p. 617.

6. *Ibid.,* p. 437 (against Kant).

7. *Ibid.,* p. 617.

8. Or " emerges " (*ibid.,* pp. 633 f.).

9. Is there perhaps expressed in this a devaluation, which is quite widespread in mythical thinking, of the profane, everyday reality, as opposed to that primordial reality, which is spoken of in myth and carried out in the cult in order to draw profane existence, which is unholy in itself, into it?

10. Heinrich Barth, *Philosophie der Erscheinung,* I, p. 10.

11. *Ibid.,* p. 11.

12. Whatever else the *archē* may be, it must in any case be *being,* in order to be the origin and the unity of all things (ὄντα).